# A KNOCK AT MIDNIGHT

"We must draw strength from the deep reservoir of Dr. King's wisdom. It is midnight, but dawn is coming. There is a 'Knock at Midnight' in every age, every decade. We can and must respond."

**—Reverend Dr. Otis Moss, Jr.**

"It is good for us, at this moment, to hear the melodious voice of a man who had the propensity to reach beyond his days and impact generations. As we reflect upon his memory, we cannot resist the temptation to measure how far we have come and thereby see how far we have to go."

**—Bishop T. D. Jakes, Sr.**

"A grateful world gave him the Nobel Peace Prize, a national holiday, and imprinted him forever on the conscience of humanity."

**—Reverend C. T. Vivian**

"Martin's range is from the earth to the heavens and throughout the whole universe, and he brings it all back in a simple way to the difficult life that all must live in our troubled world. . . . These powerful sermons spoke to the inner hearts of the people who listened to them."

**—Father Theodore Hesburgh**

"I am convinced that Martin's faith in the precious, embracing, amazing love of God was rewarded. . . . Several years after his death I saw my friend in a dream. 'It's all right, Vincent. It is well with my soul.' Somehow that message seemed large enough for me, for all of us, forever."

**—Dr. Vincent Harding**

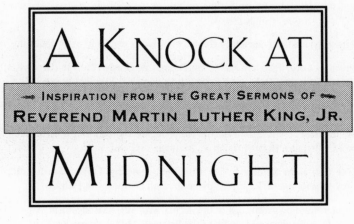

# A Knock at

### Inspiration from the Great Sermons of
### Reverend Martin Luther King, Jr.

# Midnight

### EDITED BY CLAYBORNE CARSON
### & PETER HOLLORAN

**IPM**

INTELLECTUAL PROPERTIES MANAGEMENT, INC.

### IN ASSOCIATION WITH

**WARNER BOOKS**

A Time Warner Company

Permission has been graciously granted to include excerpts from the following:

"Precious Lord, Take My Hand," by Thomas A. Dorsey. © 1938 (Renewed) Warner-Tamerlane Publishing Corp. All Rights for the World Outside U.S.A. controlled by Unichappell Music Inc. All Rights Reserved. Used by permission of Warner Bros. Publications U.S. Inc., Miami, FL 33014

"Be the Best of Whatever You Are," by Douglas Malloch. © 1926 The Scott Dowd Company. © 1954 Helen M. Malloch, renewed.

"If I Can Help Somebody." © Copyright 1944 by Lafluer Music Ltd., Copyright Renewed. Reprinted by permission of Boosey & Hawkes, Inc.

Sermons used by permission of Intellectual Properties Management, Atlanta, Georgia, as Exclusive Manager of the Estate of Martin Luther King, Jr.

Copyright information continued on page 234.

Warner Books, Inc., 1271 Avenue of the Americas, New York, NY 10020

Visit our Web site at www.twbookmark.com

**w** A Time Warner Company

First Trade Printing: January 2000

10 9 8 7 6 5 4 3 2 1

ISBN: 0-446-67554-7
LC: 98-84358

*Book design by L & G McRee*
*Cover design by Mario Pulice*
*Cover photo by Don Uhrbrock-Life*

Executive Producer: Phillip Jones

# CONTENTS

INTRODUCTION by Clayborne Carson and
Peter Holloran  vii

REDISCOVERING LOST VALUES  1
*Introduction by Dr. Wyatt Tee Walker*

PAUL'S LETTER TO AMERICAN CHRISTIANS  21
*Introduction by Reverend Dr. C. T. Vivian*

LOVING YOUR ENEMIES  37
*Introduction by Reverend Dr. Joan Brown Campbell*

A KNOCK AT MIDNIGHT  61
*Introduction by Reverend Dr. Otis Moss, Jr.*

THE AMERICAN DREAM  79
*Introduction by Bishop T. D. Jakes, Sr.*

GUIDELINES FOR A CONSTRUCTIVE CHURCH  101
*Introduction by Reverend Floyd H. Flake*

THE THREE DIMENSIONS OF A COMPLETE LIFE  117
*Introduction by Father Theodore Hesburgh*

WHY JESUS CALLED A MAN A FOOL  141
*Introduction by Reverend Billy Graham*

# CONTENTS

THE DRUM MAJOR INSTINCT      165
*Introduction by Reverend Robert M. Franklin*

UNFULFILLED DREAMS      187
*Introduction by Dr. Vincent Harding*

REMAINING AWAKE THROUGH A GREAT REVOLUTION    201
*Introduction by Archbishop Desmond Tutu*

MATERIAL OMITTED FROM THE SERMONS      225

ACKNOWLEDGMENTS      231

# INTRODUCTION

he world saw him as a marching protest leader, but Martin Luther King, Jr., was first and foremost a preacher. "In the quiet recesses of my heart," he once remarked, "I am fundamentally a clergyman, a Baptist preacher." King saw his religious identity as his "being" and "heritage," his inheritance as the "son of a Baptist preacher, the grandson of a Baptist preacher, and the great-grandson of a Baptist preacher."[1]

The remarkable sermons in this volume bear the imprint of King's strong family ties to African-American religious traditions. King's own ancestors were powerful preachers who were dedicated to challenging the status quo. His great-grandfather Willis Williams began preaching in antebellum Georgia and witnessed the emergence of independent black Baptist congregations after the Civil War. In 1894 his grandfather A. D.

Williams accepted the call to a small, struggling congregation in Atlanta, and under his leadership Ebenezer Baptist Church became a bedrock of the thriving Auburn Avenue community. In 1895 the Reverend Williams was among the founders of the National Baptist Convention, the largest African-American organization. After Williams's death in 1931, his widow, Jennie Celeste Parks Williams, used her influence to ensure that her son-in-law became Ebenezer's new pastor. The Reverend Martin Luther King, Sr. (widely known later as "Daddy King") guided the church during the difficult years of the Great Depression and would in time become even more prominent than his father-in-law in national Baptist circles.

From the time of his birth in 1929 until his death in 1968, Ebenezer was often at the center of Martin Luther King, Jr.'s, world. For a few years after graduate school King was pastor of another church in another state, but it wasn't long before the church of his ancestors called him to its pulpit, which he shared with his father for the last eight years of his life. As King explained in an autobiographical sketch written in early adulthood, Ebenezer was his second home, a place where religion was "knitted to life." The home where he spent his first twelve years was just a block up Auburn Avenue from the church. Purchased early in the century by the Reverend Williams, it was a nurturing environment, dominated during King's childhood by the "saintly" presence of the widowed Jennie Celeste

Williams. Her death in 1941 was the traumatic event of King's childhood; his parents' reassurance that she still lived strengthened his enduring belief in immortality. In his sketch, King acknowledged how his attitudes were profoundly shaped by a "real" father "who always put his family first" and a mother "behind the scene setting forth those motherly cares, the lack of which leaves a missing link in life." These family influences contributed to King's sense of religious optimism: "It is quite easy for me to think of a God of love mainly because I grew up in a family where love was central and where lovely relationships were ever present."[2]

King's own social activism was built upon the social gospel Christianity of his grandfather and father. Williams had been a founder of the Atlanta NAACP branch, and the senior King continued his predecessor's civil rights activism. The younger King recalled that his father refused to ride segregated city buses and led the NAACP fight to bring black teachers' salaries to the level of white teachers' during the 1930s. King, Jr.'s understanding of the Baptist ministry grew from his admiration for his ancestors' dual concern with individual salvation and the pressing needs of the Atlanta black community. In a 1940 sermon to other clergymen, for example, King, Sr., was unapologetic about his activism. The church, he said, must "touch every phase of community life." Citing a biblical passage that both father and son would use to ignite a fiery sermon, King, Sr., declared that "quite often we say the church has no place in politics, forgetting the words of the Lord, 'The spirit of the Lord is upon me, because he hath anointed me to preach the Gospel to the poor; he hath sent me to heal the brokenhearted, to preach deliverance to the captives, and the recovering of sight to the blind, to set at liberty them that are bruised.' "[3]

Despite a strong anchor of faith and his belief in the church's mission, King, Jr., experienced a period of religious skepticism during his teenage years and later expressed discomfort over emotionalism in religious practice. He recalled wondering whether the church could "be intellectually respectable as well as emotionally satisfying" and "serve as a vehicle to modern thinking."[4] King gradually came to accept his religious calling after entering Morehouse College at the age of fifteen. "I came to see that God had placed a responsibility upon my shoulders and the more I tried to escape it the more frustrated I would become," he later explained. His father's "noble example" was "the great moving factor" supporting his decision to enter the ministry.[5] In addition, Morehouse president Benjamin Mays and religion professor George Kelsey provided examples of men who were devout, yet also learned. "I could see in their lives the ideal of what I wanted a minister to be."[6] Mays in particular encouraged King's sense of Christian mission and his interest in Gandhian nonviolence. In February 1948, during his senior year at Morehouse, he was ordained at Ebenezer by ministers who had known him since his youth.

That fall he entered Crozer Theological Seminary

enthusiastic about liberal Christianity, but he soon acknowledged its limitations, particularly its faith in human goodness. As he explained in one of his seminary papers, his awareness of the South's "vicious race problem" undermined his liberal optimism by making "it very difficult . . . to believe in the essential goodness of man."[7] King approached his theological studies with great seriousness, always searching for ways to apply theological understanding to his pastoral needs. An eclectic rather than original religious thinker, he mined European-American theological texts for nuggets of insight that would enrich his preaching without stultifying it. King's graduate studies in systematic theology at Boston University further deepened his theological understanding and marked his arrival among the elite ministers who held doctorates. Recruited for several teaching positions, King was drawn to the pulpit instead, and to his native South.

"Rediscovering Lost Values," the earliest of the eleven sermons included in this volume, was delivered in February 1954 at Detroit's Second Baptist Church while King was still at graduate student at Boston University. His earliest recorded sermon, it demonstrates the oratorical power he had acquired while still a young man. "I'm not going to put my ultimate faith in the little gods that can be destroyed in an atomic age," King declared, "but the God who has been our help in the ages past." King's willingness to challenge an audience composed mainly of his elders is striking. Identifying the moral decay at the center of modern life,

King prescribed an abiding faith and an ethical life as the only cures. "The thing that we need in the world today is a group of men and women who will stand up for right and be opposed to wrong, wherever it is."

Shortly after King delivered "Rediscovering," Dexter Avenue Baptist Church in Montgomery, Alabama, called him to its pulpit. He approached his new role with exceptional confidence, born of a lifetime's familiarity with preachers and congregations. Deeply influenced by other great religious leaders of his time, King's preaching bore the imprint not only of his father and grandfather, but of his Morehouse mentor Mays; of Crozer professor George W. Davis; of theologian Howard Thurman, who befriended King in Boston; of Vernon Johns, his idiosyncratic predecessor at Dexter; of Harry Emerson Fosdick of New York's Riverside Church; and of many other ministers who kept the social gospel tradition alive during the Cold War era. He created a file that would contain each of the sermons in his repertory, along with related articles and biblical explications that he could adapt for his purposes. Borrowing ideas from other preachers, King transformed his source materials in distinctive ways. By the time he accepted Dexter's call, he had developed a rich repertoire of quotations, stories, and set pieces that could be called forth for any occasion. His favorite sermons would assume different forms as he reworked them and as his storehouse of homiletic devices diversified. By the end of his life King was still using some set pieces, like the interdependence of humanity when sitting down to breakfast, that he had developed during his early years as a preacher. He had become more willing, though, to tell stories from his own life and the lives of his congregation.

King's sermons at Dexter and later at Ebenezer Church reflected his Baptist affiliation, but they also expressed universal, ecumenical values rather than a denominational creed. He devoted less attention to individual redemption and salvation than to the social message of Jesus. King's version of the Christian message applied to the affairs of this world as well as to the afterlife. He conveyed God's judgment of contemporary institutions, especially churches and political institutions. The New Testament gave him the expectation of ultimate forgiveness for our sins; the Old Testament the assurance that God acted on behalf of good.

"Loving Your Enemies" was among the first sermons he ever gave at Dexter Avenue Baptist Church, although the earliest recorded version dates from a few years later, when King decided to preach it at Dexter for a third time. Few sermons express so well King's fundamental religious values. In 1954, when the Dexter congregation heard this sermon for the first time, King emphasized the Christian basis for resisting evil. By the time he delivered the sermon published here he had become a symbol of Gandhian nonviolent resistance, but the Sermon on the Mount remained the focus of his sermon rather than Gandhi. King would often return to the sermon text from the book of

Matthew: "But I say unto you, Love your enemies, bless them that curse you, do good to them that hate you, and pray for them which despitefully use you, and persecute you." "The redemptive power of love" became the basis of King's argument for the ultimate triumph of good: "And when we discover [that power] we will be able to make of this old world a new world."

In December 1955 the Montgomery bus boycott movement thrust King into a role in which he could display his exceptional leadership abilities. As a civil rights leader he spoke out on secular issues and became firmly attached to a Gandhian strategy of nonviolence. He never abandoned his conviction, though, that Christian principles provided a necessary foundation for the African-American freedom struggle. His pastoral practice prepared him for his public ministry. Like his formal sermons, many of his speeches at mass meetings were delivered in churches and utilized biblical texts. They combined spiritual inspiration and social analysis, careful preparation and extemporaneous insightfulness.

The bus boycott brought King's oratorical brilliance to the nation's attention, and some of the sermons included in this volume were delivered in response to the many invitations that King received during his career as a protest leader. They indicate his development as a religious leader and reveal his efforts to apply Christian teachings to the major issues of his time and ours. Most are being released in audio for the first time; nearly half make their first appearance in print here.

Transcribing King's recorded sermons, particularly those with such a rich call-and-response interaction between preacher and congregation, is a delicate task. Over the last decade the Martin Luther King, Jr., Papers Project has developed a set of editorial principles for transcribing King's sermons, including audiorecordings. Those principles generally informed the transcriptions included here, though considerations of clarity and consistency required a few modifications. The method developed by the King Papers Project enables the reader to gauge the congregation's reaction to King's words; the congregation's responses are italicized and enclosed in parentheses. For more details regarding transcription practices, see the project's edition of *The Papers of Martin Luther King, Jr.*

"Paul's Letter to American Christians" galvanized thousands of delegates—including King's father, mother, and other relatives—attending the 1956 National Baptist Convention held in Denver. According to an account of that event, his delivery "started slowly and never gained speed or volume, but it gripped and held this audience of ten thousand or more. . . . We hung over the balcony rail and wept unashamedly. When he quietly announced the pro forma 'I must close now,' the sea of black Baptists arose as one and protested."[8] Family friend J. Pius Barbour declared that King "just wrapped the convention up in a napkin and carried it away in his pocket." He expressed pride that the young Crozer student he had known had "grown TWENTY YEARS in about five." He proclaimed

King "the greatest orator on the American platform," effusing that King was "the first Ph.D. I have heard that can make uneducated people throw their hats in the air over philosophy."[9] It undoubtedly received a more measured response from the restrained Dexter congregation, which heard the version included here several months later. In this sermon King audaciously assumes the role of the Apostle Paul in order to denounce the excesses of capitalism, materialism, and sectarianism in twentieth-century America. Never explicitly referring to nonviolence, he nevertheless emphasizes its fundamental tenets using Christian symbols and imagery. He urges those struggling against oppression to use "Christian methods and Christian weapons," especially the weapon of love.

King preached "A Knock at Midnight" on many occasions both before and after he chose it for publication in his first book of sermons, *Strength to Love*, which appeared in 1963. It develops some of the themes of social criticism that were suggested in "Rediscovering Lost Values," but by the 1960s King's commentary had become more pointed and increasingly controversial. Midnight exists not only in the external social order but in our internal psychological and moral life. He finds the Christian church itself wanting because of its failure to challenge the status quo, yet the church is nevertheless important. "The bread of life is there."

"The American Dream" is another oft-given sermon that King adapted to many occasions during the

1960s. Based on secular texts of the American democratic tradition rather than the Bible, it is not a traditional sermon. He nevertheless uses these nontraditional texts to develop some of the central themes of his ministry. He sees the nation's democratic experiment as a test of its spiritual convictions. For King, the essence of democracy is the belief that each person is created in the image of God. "We will know one day that God made us to live together as brothers and to respect the dignity and worth of every man," he affirms.

As his father had challenged churchmen to live up to their social responsibilities, so too did King pose similar challenges in "Guidelines for a Constructive Church," delivered in 1966 at Ebenezer Baptist Church. Urging all Christians to think about more than ultimate redemption, King conveys the central themes of social gospel Christianity and concisely identifies the broad range of his concerns regarding issues of personal ethics, social justice, and peace.

King delivered "The Three Dimensions of a Complete Life" as a trial sermon during his first visit to Dexter Avenue Baptist Church, and it remained one of his most accessible sermons. Like he did with his other sermons, he borrowed its simple structure from another preacher. But on this scaffolding he hung his own ideas. In this sermon King pushes listeners from a self-centered concern with their personal welfare ("the length of life") toward concern for the welfare of others ("the breath of life") and finally toward confrontation with God ("the height of life"). More than fifteen years after first developing this sermon, King had become so familiar with it that it became a marvelous vehicle for reflecting on his own life. The mature version included here—like half of the sermons in this volume, this is its first time in print—was delivered in April 1967 at Chicago's New Covenant Baptist Church, a friendly and talkative church. Few of King's sermons are as dramatic and self-assured as this version of his flagship sermon.

Another Chicago sermon, "Why Jesus Called a Man a Fool," delivered in August 1967, allowed King to explain the connection between his ministry and his civil rights activism. "Before I was a civil rights leader, I was a preacher of the gospel," he reminds the congregation. "This was my first calling and it still remains my greatest commitment." He addresses the criticisms he faced from fundamentalist ministers by arguing that preachers must be concerned with "the whole man—not merely his soul but his body." King proceeds to challenge the materialism of his listeners and their failure to recognize their dependence on others and on God.

"The Drum Major Instinct" is perhaps King's best-known sermon. Delivered at Ebenezer just two months before his death, it is certainly one of his most personal, merging his homiletic intentions with a measure of self-criticism. King clearly understood his susceptibility to the ego's own need for praise and esteem. The sermon ends with his own famous eulogy that summarizes his fatalistic sense of mission: "I'd like somebody to mention that day that Martin Luther King, Jr., tried to give his life serving others."

King's reflections regarding his own partially fulfilled goals provide the theme for "Unfulfilled Dreams," delivered at Ebenezer in March 1968. Aware of the difficulty of achieving his social justice goals and enduring intense public criticisms because of his controversial statements, King found solace in the fact that Gandhi and Woodrow Wilson and the Apostle Paul also failed to achieve their final objectives. Throughout his life, King responded to setbacks and frustrations by looking to God for support. "I heard the voice of Jesus saying still to fight on. He promised never to leave me, never to leave me alone."

King's final sermon, "Remaining Awake Through a Great Revolution," was delivered on many occasions but never more effectively than at the end of King's life. Delivered at Washington's National Cathedral during the final days of his life, it serves as King's concluding statement on the great issues of his time: racial equality, economic justice, and peace. Developing ideas that he had expressed on many previous occasions, King rejects the role of "consensus" leader in order to assert his opposition to the Vietnam War. Speaking near the seat of government, King proclaims: "I believe there is a need for all people of goodwill to come with a massive act of conscience and say in the words of the old Negro spiritual, 'We ain't gonna study war no more.'"

Taken together, King's great sermons illustrate the

evolution of his religious beliefs as well as his preaching style as he confronted the issues of his time and of ours. More than three decades after they were delivered, his sermons still stand as a profound testament to his prophetic leadership of the struggle against racial and economic oppression.

# NOTES

1. "The Un-Christian Christian: SCLC Looks Closely at Christianity in a Troubled Land," in *Ebony* 20 (August 1965), p. 76.

2. This and other autobiographical quotations are from King's "Autobiography of Religious Development," written in 1951 and reprinted in Clayborne Carson, Ralph E. Luker, and Penny A. Russell, eds., *The Papers of Martin Luther King, Jr., Volume I: January 1929–June 1951* (Berkeley: University of California Press, 1992), pp. 359–363.

3. Quoted in *Papers I*, p. 34.

4. Quoted in "Attack on the Conscience," *Time*, 18 February 1957, p. 18.

5. Quoted in *Papers I*, p. 45.

6. Quoted in William Peters, " 'Our Weapon is Love,' " in *Redbook* 107 (August 1956), p. 42.

7. King, "How Modern Christians Should Think of Man," in *Papers I*, p. 274.

8. Henry H. Mitchell, "The Awesome Meek," in *Pulpit Digest*, January–February 1991.

9. Barbour, "Sermons and Addresses at the Convention," in *National Baptist Voice*, September 1956.

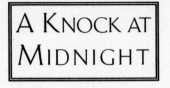

A KNOCK AT MIDNIGHT

# REDISCOVERING LOST VALUES

INTRODUCTION BY DR. WYATT TEE WALKER

This sermon by Martin Luther King, Jr., is *very early King*, is pre-Montgomery *King*. The message is carefully crafted and theologically sound, but does not yet reflect the maturity thrust upon this towering social prophet of the twentieth century by the cauldron of struggle of the Montgomery Bus Protest. Montgomery's significance was twofold: It was the first time nonviolence had been employed on a mass scale, and it marked the first time it was used on a mass scale in United States race relations.

In "Rediscovering Lost Values" Dr. King demonstrates the pronounced highly ethical and moral dynamic that propelled his ministry and movement as the moral leader of the United States in this century. King's overriding concern was this: *Is our movement right and moral*? Throughout my long association with Dr. King, it was always arresting to notice his devotion to reconciliation and not victory. This sermon was a launching pad to his keen awareness of the pervasive moral dilemma of the West and the world. It reveals the fine-tuning of his natural intellectual prowess through the skillful use of the Hegelian dialectic in the construction of the sermon itself. There is not yet the florid style that characterized his post-Montgomery preaching, though there are brief flashes that suggest that florid style was in incubation in the young preacher. This sermon is marked by an economy of King's later expressiveness in relation to substantive and concrete ideas, with which the hearers must wrestle individually and collectively depending on their respective faith commitments. His metaphors are clear and straightforward: jumping off a tall building in Detroit and the catalog of the universality of the immorality of hatred. The injection of sparingly used humor later became a Kingian trademark (although Martin Luther King, Jr., was intensely serious about his preaching craft and would not allow himself the slightest temptation of being confused with an entertainer).

The strength of this sermon is that it is as relevant and timely in 1998 as it was on February 28, 1954. As we approach the twenty-first century, how desperately this world needs to rediscover that *all reality hinges on moral foundations* and that *there is a God in the process* of all reality. The persuasiveness of King's preaching style is evident in that he appeals to the mind as well as the heart. The legendary Phillips Brooks is reported to have defined preaching as the proclamation of truth through personality. Dr. King's preaching gifts are faithful to that definition, for his preaching, early and late, reveals a marvelous wedding of passion and intellect.

Some years ago, John Ansbro and his colleagues were developing what became an interesting though imprecise philosophical biography of Dr. King. In the course of pursuing their inquiry, they asked this writer, Whose writings influenced Martin Luther King, Jr., most? My answer was Matthew, Mark, Luke, and John! Ansbro confessed that with more than a score of interviews of King's teachers and close associates, no one had offered a similar reply. The basis of Martin Luther King's ministry and mission was the ethics and morality of the Crucified Carpenter from Galilee. This early sermon validates that assessment, as do all of his later efforts.

Despite the now legendary oratorical gifts that King developed in his post-Montgomery career, first and foremost he was an unapologetic proclaimer of the Gospel of Jesus of Nazareth.

---

DR. WYATT TEE WALKER is former Chief of Staff to Dr. King and for the last thirty years he has served as Senior Pastor of the Canaan Baptist Church of Christ in Harlem, New York. Dr. Walker holds an earned doctorate in music and ethnographic history and is the author of nineteen books.

# Rediscovering
# Lost Values

I want you to think with me this morning from the subject: "Rediscovering Lost Values." There is something wrong with our world, something fundamentally and basically wrong. I don't think we have to look too far to see that. I'm sure that most of you would agree with me in making that assertion. And when we stop to analyze the cause of our world's ills, many things come to mind.

We begin to wonder if it is due to the fact that we don't know enough. But it can't be that. Because in terms of accumulated knowledge we know more today than men have known in any period of human history. We have the facts at our disposal. We know more about mathematics, about science, about social science, and philosophy than we've ever known in any period of the world's history. So it can't be because we don't know enough.

And then we wonder if it is due to the fact that our scientific genius lags behind. That is, if we have not made enough progress scientifically. Well then, it can't be that. For our scientific progress over the past years has been amazing. Man through his scientific genius has been able to dwarf distance and place time in chains, so that today it's possible to eat breakfast in New York City and supper in London, England. Back in about 1753 it took a letter three days to go from New York City to Washington, and today you can go from here to China in less time than that. It can't be because man is stagnant in his scientific progress. Man's scientific genius has been amazing.

I think we have to look much deeper than that if we are to find the real cause of man's problems and the real cause of the world's ills today. If we are to really find it I think we will have to look in the hearts and souls of men. (*Lord help him*)

The trouble isn't so much that we don't know enough, but it's as if we aren't good enough. The trouble isn't so much that our scientific genius lags behind, but our moral genius lags behind. (*Well*) The great problem facing modern man is that the means by which we live (*Help him God*) have outdistanced the spiritual ends for which we live. (*That's right*) So we find ourselves caught in a messed-up world. (*Well*) The problem is with man himself and man's soul. We haven't learned how to be just and honest and kind and true and loving. And that is the basis of our problem. The real problem is that through our scientific genius we've made of the world a neighborhood, but through our moral and spiritual genius we've failed to make of it a brotherhood. (*Lord have mercy*) And the great danger facing us today is not so much the atomic bomb that was created by physical science. Not so much that atomic bomb that you can put in an airplane and drop on the heads of hundreds and thousands of people—as dangerous as that is. But the real danger confronting civilization today is that atomic bomb which lies in the hearts and souls of men, (*Lord have mercy*) capable of exploding into the vilest of hate and into the most damaging selfishness—that's the atomic bomb that we've got to fear today. (*Lord help him*) Problem is with the men. (*Yes, yes*) Within the heart and the souls of men. (*Lord*) That is the real basis of our problem. (*Well*)

My friends, all I'm trying to say is that if we are to go forward today, we've got to go back and rediscover some mighty precious values that we've left behind. (*Yes*) That's the only way that we would be able to make of our world a better world, and to make of this world what God wants it to be and the real purpose and meaning of it. The only way we can do it is to go back (*Yes*) and rediscover some mighty precious values that we've left behind.

Our situation in the world today reminds me of a very popular situation that took place in the life of Jesus. It was read in the Scripture for the morning, found over in the second chapter of Luke's gospel. The story is very familiar, very popular; we all know it. You remember when Jesus was about twelve years old, (*Well*) there was the custom of the feast. Jesus' parents took him up to Jerusalem. That was an annual occasion, the feast of the Passover, and they went up to Jerusalem and they took Jesus along with them. And they were there a few days, and then after being there they decided to go back home, to Nazareth. (*Lord help him*) And they started out, and I guess as it was in the tradition in those days, the father probably traveled in front, and then the mother and the children behind. You see, they didn't have the modern conveniences that we have today. They didn't have automobiles and subways and buses. They walked, and traveled on donkeys and camels and what have you. So they traveled very slow, but it was usually the tradition for the father to lead the way. (*Yeah*)

And they left Jerusalem going on back to Nazareth, and I imagine they walked a little while and they didn't look back to see if everybody was there. But then the Scripture says, they went about a day's journey and they stopped, I imagine to check up, to see if everything was all right, and they discovered that something mighty precious was missing. They discovered that Jesus wasn't with them. (*Yes*) Jesus wasn't in the midst. (*Come on*) And so they paused there and looked and they didn't see him around. And they went on and started looking among the kinsfolk. And they went on back to Jerusalem and found him there, in the temple with the doctors of the law. (*Yeah, that's right*)

Now, the real thing that is to be seen here is this: that the parents of Jesus realized that they had left, and that they had lost a mighty precious value. They had sense enough to know that before they could go forward to Nazareth, they had to go backward to Jerusalem to rediscover this value. (*That's right*) They knew that. They knew that they couldn't go home to Nazareth until they went back to Jerusalem. (*Come on*)

Sometimes, you know, it's necessary to go backward in order to go forward. (*Yes*) That's an analogy of life. I remember the other day I was driving out of New York City into Boston, and I stopped off in Bridgeport, Connecticut, to visit some friends. And I went out of New York on a highway that's known as the Merritt Parkway, it leads into Boston, a very fine parkway. And I stopped in Bridgeport, and after being there for two or three hours I decided to go on to Boston, and I wanted to get back on the Merritt Parkway. And I went out thinking that I was going toward the Merritt Parkway. I started out, and I rode, and I kept riding, and I looked up and I saw a sign saying two miles to a little town that I knew I was to bypass—I wasn't to pass through that particular town. So I thought I was on the wrong road. I stopped and I asked a gentleman on the road which way would I get to the Merritt Parkway. And he said, "The Merritt Parkway is about twelve or fifteen miles back that way. You've got to turn around and go back to the Merritt Parkway; you are out of the way now." In other words, before I could go forward to Boston, I had to go back about twelve or fifteen miles to get to the Merritt Parkway. May it not be that modern man has gotten on the wrong parkway? (*Lord help him*) And if he is to go forward to the city of salvation, he's got to go back and get on the right parkway. (*Amen*)

And so that was the thing that Jesus' parents realized, that they had to go back and find this mighty precious value that they had left behind, in order to go forward. They realized that. And so they went back to Jerusalem and discovered Jesus, rediscovered him so to speak, in order to go forward to Nazareth. (*Lord help him*)

Now that's what we've got to do in our world today. We've left a lot of precious values behind; we've lost a lot of precious values. And if we are to go forward, if we are to make this a better world in which to live, we've got to go back. We've got to rediscover these precious values that we've left behind.

I want to deal with one or two of these mighty precious values that we've left behind, that if we're to go forward and to make this a better world, we must rediscover.

The first is this—the first principle of value that we need to rediscover is this: that all reality hinges on moral foundations. In other words, that this is a moral universe, and that there are moral laws of the universe just as abiding as the physical laws. (*Lord help us*) I'm not so sure we all believe that. We never doubt that there are physical laws of the universe that we must obey. We never doubt that. And so we just don't jump out of airplanes or jump off of high buildings for the fun of it—we don't do that. Because we unconsciously know that there is a final law of gravitation, and if you disobey it you'll suffer the consequences—we know that. Even if we don't know it in its Newtonian formulation, we know it intuitively, and so we just don't jump off the highest building in Detroit for the fun of it—we don't do that. Because we know that there is a law of gravitation which is final in the universe. (*Lord*) If we disobey it we'll suffer the consequences.

But I'm not so sure if we know that there are moral laws just as abiding as the physical law. I'm not so sure about that. I'm not so sure if we really believe that there is a law of love in this universe, and that if you disobey it you'll suffer the consequences. (*Yes*) I'm not so sure if we really believe that. Now at least two things convince me that we don't believe that, that we have strayed away from the principle that this is a moral universe. (*Lord help him*)

The first thing is that we have adopted in the modern world a sort of a relativistic ethic. Now I'm not trying to use a big word here; I'm trying to say something very concrete. And that is that we have accepted the attitude that right and wrong are merely relative . . .*

Most people can't stand up for their convictions, because the majority of people might not be doing it. (*Amen, yes*) See, everybody's not doing it, so it must be wrong. And since everybody is doing it, it must be right. (*Yes, Lord help him*) So [it's] a sort of numerical interpretation of what's right.

But I'm here to say to you this morning that some

*Recording interrupted.

things are right and some things are wrong. (*Yes*) Eternally so, absolutely so. It's wrong to hate. (*Yes, that's right*) It always has been wrong and it always will be wrong. (*Amen*) It's wrong in America, it's wrong in Germany, it's wrong in Russia, it's wrong in China. (*Lord help him*) It was wrong in 2000 B.C., and it's wrong in 1954 A.D. It always has been wrong, (*That's right*) and it always will be wrong. (*That's right*) It's wrong to throw our lives away in riotous living. (*Yeah*) No matter if everybody in Detroit is doing it, it's wrong. (*Yes*) It always will be wrong, and it always has been wrong. It's wrong in every age and it's wrong in every nation. Some things are right and some things are wrong, no matter if everybody is doing the contrary. Some things in this universe are absolute. The God of the universe has made it so. And so long as we adopt this relative attitude toward right and wrong, we're revolting against the very laws of God himself. (*Amen*)

Now that isn't the only thing that convinces me that we've strayed away from this attitude, (*Go ahead*) this principle. The other thing is that we have adopted a sort of pragmatic test for right and wrong—whatever works is right. (*Yes*) If it works, it's all right. Nothing is wrong but that which does not work. If you don't get caught, it's right. [*Laughter*] That's the attitude, isn't it? It's all right to disobey the Ten Commandments, but just don't disobey the eleventh, "Thou shall not get caught." [*Laughter*] That's the attitude. That's the prevailing attitude in our culture. (*Come on*) No matter

what you do, just do it with a bit of finesse. (*All right*)
You know, a sort of attitude of the survival of the slickest. Not the Darwinian survival of the fittest, but the
survival of the slickest—whoever can be the slickest is
the one who [is] right. It's all right to lie, but lie with
dignity. [*Laughter*] It's all right to steal and to rob and
extort, but do it with a bit of finesse. (*Yes*) It's even all
right to hate, but just dress your hate up in the garments of love and make it appear that you are loving
when you are actually hating. Just get by! That's the
thing that's right according to this new ethic. (*Lord
help him*)

My friends, that attitude is destroying the soul of
our culture. (*You're right there*) It's destroying our nation. (*Oh yes*) The thing that we need in the world
today is a group of men and women who will stand up
for right and to be opposed to wrong, wherever it is.
(*Lord have mercy*) A group of people who have come to
see that some things are wrong, whether they're never
caught up with. And some things are right, whether
nobody sees you doing them or not.

All I'm trying to say to you is (*Have mercy, my God*)
that our world hinges on moral foundations. God has
made it so. God has made the universe to be based on
a moral law. (*Lord help him*) So long as man disobeys
it he is revolting against God. That's what we need in
the world today: people who will stand for right and
goodness. It's not enough to know the intricacies of zo-
ology and biology, but we must know the intricacies of
law. (*Well*) It is not enough to know that two and two

makes four, but we've got to know somehow that it's right to be honest and just with our brothers. (*Yes*) It's not enough to know all about our philosophical and mathematical disciplines, (*Have mercy*) but we've got to know the simple disciplines of being honest and loving and just with all humanity. (*Oh yes*) If we don't learn it, we will destroy ourselves (*That's right*) by the misuse of our own powers. (*Amen*)

This universe hinges on moral foundations. (*Yeah*) There is something in this universe that justifies Carlyle in saying "No lie can live forever." There is something in this universe that justifies William Cullen Bryant in saying "Truth, crushed to earth, will rise again." (*My Lord, amen*) There is something in this universe that justifies James Russell Lowell in saying

Truth forever on the scaffold,
Wrong forever on the throne.
Yet that scaffold sways the future. (*Lord help him*)
Behind the dim unknown stands God,
Within the shadow keeping watch above his own.
  (*Amen*)

There is something in this universe that justifies the biblical writer in saying "You shall reap what you sow." (*Amen*) This is a law-abiding universe. (*Amen*) This is a moral universe. It hinges on moral foundations. (*Lord help him*) If we are to make of this a better world, we've got to go back and rediscover that precious value that we've left behind. (*Yes*)

And then there is a second thing, a second principle that we've got to go back and rediscover. (*Help him*) And that is that all reality has spiritual control. In other words, we've got to go back and rediscover the principle that there is a God behind the process. Well, this you say: "Why is it that you raise that as a point in your sermon, in a church? The mere fact we are at church, we believe in God, we don't need to go back and rediscover that. The mere fact that we are here, and the mere fact that we sing and pray, and come to church—we believe in God." Well, there's some truth in that. But we must remember that it's possible to affirm the existence of God with your lips and deny his existence with your life. (*Amen, preach*) The most dangerous type of atheism is not theoretical atheism but practical atheism (*Amen*)—that's the most dangerous type. (*Lord have mercy*) And the world, even the church, is filled up with people who pay lip service to God and not life service. (*That's right. Filled up with. Come on, Lord help him*) And there is always a danger that we will make it appear externally that we believe in God when internally we don't. (*Yes*) We say with our mouths that we believe in him, but we live with our lives like he never existed. (*That's right*) That is the ever-present danger confronting religion. That's a dangerous type of atheism.

And I think, my friends, that that is the thing that has happened in America. That we have unconsciously left God behind. Now, we haven't consciously done it; we have unconsciously done it. You see, the text, you remember the text said that Jesus' parents went a whole day's journey not knowing that he wasn't with them. They didn't consciously leave him behind. (*Well*) It was unconscious; went a whole day and didn't even know it. It wasn't a conscious process. You see, we didn't grow up and say, "Now, goodbye God, we're going to leave you now." The materialism in America has been an unconscious thing. Since the rise of the Industrial Revolution in England, and then the invention of all of our gadgets and contrivances and all of the things and modern conveniences—we unconsciously left God behind. We didn't mean to do it.

We just became so involved in getting our big bank accounts that we unconsciously forgot about God—we didn't mean to do it.

We became so involved in getting our nice luxurious cars, and they're very nice, but we became so involved in it that it became much more convenient to ride out to the beach on Sunday afternoon than to come to church that morning. (*Yes*) It was an unconscious thing—we didn't mean to do it.

We became so involved and fascinated by the intricacies of television that we found it a little more convenient to stay at home than to come to church. It was an unconscious thing—we didn't mean to do it. We didn't just go up and say, "Now God, we're gone." (*Lord help him*) We had gone a whole day's journey, (*Yes*) and then we came to see that we had unconsciously ushered God out of the universe. A whole day's journey—didn't mean to do it. We just became so involved in things that we forgot about God. (*Oh yes*)

And that is the danger confronting us, my friends: that in a nation as ours where we stress mass production, and that's mighty important, where we have so many conveniences and luxuries and all of that, there is the danger that we will unconsciously forget about God. I'm not saying that these things aren't important; we need them, we need cars, we need money; all of that's important to live. But whenever they become substitutes for God, (*Yes*) they become injurious. (*Amen*)

And may I say to you this morning (*Lord help him*) that none of these things can ever be real substitutes for God. Automobiles and subways, televisions and radios, dollars and cents can never be substitutes for God. (*Amen*) For long before any of these came into existence, we needed God. (*Amen, yes*) And long after they will have passed away, we will still need God. (*Oh yeah*)

And I say to you this morning in conclusion (*Lord have mercy*) that I'm not going to put my ultimate faith in things. I'm not going to put my ultimate faith in gadgets and contrivances. As a young man with most of my life ahead of me, I decided early (*Oh yeah*) to give my life to something eternal and absolute. (*All right*) Not to these little gods that are here today and gone tomorrow, (*Come on*) but to God who is the same yesterday, today, and forever. (*Amen, amen*)

Not in the little gods that can be with us in a few moments of prosperity, (*Yes*) but in the God who walks with us through the valley of the shadow of death (*That's right*) and causes us to fear no evil. (*All right*) That's the God. (*Come on*)

Not in the god that can give us a few Cadillac cars and Buick convertibles, as nice as they are, that are in style today and out of style three years from now, (*All right*) but the God who threw up the stars (*Come on*) to bedeck the heavens like swinging lanterns of eternity. (*All right. Oh yes*)

Not in the god that can throw up a few skyscraping buildings, but the God who threw up the gigantic mountains, kissing the sky, (*Amen*) as if to bathe their peaks in the lofty blues. (*Yes*)

Not in the god that can give us a few televisions and radios, but the God who threw up that great cosmic light that gets up early in the morning in the eastern horizon, (*Oh yes*) who paints its technicolor across the blue (*Oh yes, come on*)—something that man could never make. (*All right, yes*)

I'm not going to put my ultimate faith in the little gods that can be destroyed in an atomic age (*Yes*) but the God who has been our help in ages past, (*Come on*) and our hope for years to come, (*All right*) and our shelter in the time of storm, (*Oh yes*) and our eternal home. That's the God that I'm putting my ultimate faith in. (*Oh yes, come on now*) That's the God that I call upon you to worship this morning. (*Yes*)

Go out and be assured that that God is going to last forever. (*Yes*) Storms might come and go. (*Yes*) Our great skyscraping buildings will come and go. (*Yes*)

Our beautiful automobiles will come and go, but God will be here. (*Amen*) Plants may wither, the flowers may fade away, but the word of our God shall stand forever and nothing can ever stop him. (*Bring it down*) All of the P-38s in the world can never reach God. All of our atomic bombs can never reach him. The God that I'm talking about this morning (*Come on*) is the God of the universe and the God that will last through the ages. (*All right*) If we are to go forward this morning, (*Well*) we've got to go back and find that God. (*All right*) That is the God that demands and commands our ultimate allegiance. (*Right*)

If we are to go forward, (*Oh yes*) we must go back and rediscover these precious values: (*Well*) that all reality hinges on moral foundations (*Lord have mercy*) and that all reality has spiritual control. (*Yes*) God bless you. (*Amen, amen, amen*)

DELIVERED AT SECOND BAPTIST CHURCH, DETROIT, MICHIGAN, 28 FEBRUARY 1954 [SDBCC]

# PAUL'S LETTER TO AMERICAN CHRISTIANS

INTRODUCTION BY REVEREND DR. C. T. VIVIAN

his is among the earliest of Martin Luther King's best-known sermons. Reading it is to read the mind of Martin before he became the conscience of a nation, the leader of a people, and national spokesman for the poor.

It is most important that we always see him as minister, a preacher as well as an activist, spokesman, and civil rights leader. The latter are only expressions of his ministry. Martin changed this century's image of ministers and the ministry. He made social activism almost necessary for clergy.

Few, if any, southern pastors or politicians had an earned doctorate. Martin was prepared to minister on social issues and was better prepared than others to be a national leader. Very seldom have the poor of America had such an able spokesman to organize them. He could demand order beyond law and deliver truth to power on their behalf.

A look at the list of Nobel Prize winners reveals a startling fact: The nation has existed in a Christian civilization for centuries and as an American Christian culture since its inception, yet Dr. Martin Luther King was only the third Christian cleric to receive the highest award of Western culture: the Nobel Peace Prize.

Nor did he curry the favor of the church. As this early sermon and his later speeches reveal, he aggressively challenged the church in every possible way. Yet his love for the Faith, the truths of Jesus, and the hope to reform the church was obvious.

This sermon to the church was a declaration of the problems and possibilities of our time. Because he knew the church saw itself as the value-producing institution of a Christian culture, he first declared needs to the church. Furthermore, he would forever preach that social problems and racism in particular are moral and spiritual problems that create political and economic consequences. He wanted the church on his side, but not on its terms. His ability to reach the conscience of America would be his greatest contribution to the freedom struggles of the oppressed. From this moral and spiritual perspective, he made continuous demands on the structures—or, as Paul would say, "the principalities and powers of this world." (In some ways his Letter from a Birmingham Jail starts with his Letter to American Christians.)

In this early sermon he reaches out to all Christians by speaking of brokenness and denominational disunity. Later he would reach out to all faiths, and they would hear him more profoundly than most Christian leaders. The greatly revered Rabbi Abraham Heschel, mystic, scholar, and activist, told all who valued him, "The whole future of America will depend on the impact and influence of Dr. King." His statement remains true. Martin's movement eventually created the greatest ecumenical force in modern time.

Martin always practiced in public places what he preached in the pulpit. He demanded courage from churchmen, and he personally preached it. His courage caused him to actively challenge all systems—first the church, then political systems, and finally economic systems. His demands for justice, freedom, and jobs led to his greatest victories. Those victories taught us to believe the human community could become whatever it chooses to become. He did it by teaching us to shape legislation from the streets, not just the suites.

This sermon is an outline of his coming years of nonviolent direct-action campaigns. He chastises the church and bases his action organization, the Southern Christian Leadership Conference, in the African-American church. The Voting Rights Bill was the high point of his organized challenge to political structures. The Poor People's Campaign was the high point of his attempt to correct the excesses of the economic system and place an income floor under every family. This act of love for all people led to his martyrdom.

This sermon, preached in his Dexter Avenue Baptist Church pulpit on November 4, 1956—nine days before the Supreme Court declared Alabama bus segregation laws unconstitutional—allowed him to speak from a position of power. Throughout the year 1956 he had practiced with integrity what he preached. He would use the most powerful new force of this millennium: nonviolent direct action. Through his ministry of nonviolence he gave our complex, fragile society the answer to its central problem: how to solve social problems without violence. By so doing he further perfected our democracy, caused us to face deep racial and economic problems, and furthered our faith in the spiritual concepts that Martin believed underlie all reality.

As a result, a grateful world gave him the Nobel Peace Prize, a national holiday, and imprinted him forever on the conscience of humanity. Without intending to do so, this twentieth-century minister of Jesus Christ became our twenty-first-century prophet.

---

REVEREND DR. C. T. VIVIAN served on Dr. King's Executive Staff as national director of affiliates and has organized many nonviolent direct action campaigns. He is founder and chair of the Center for Democratic Renewal, the National Center for Human Rights Education, and his consultancy, Basic Action Strategies and Information Center.

# Paul's Letter
## to American
## Christians

I would like to share with you an imaginary letter from the pen of the Apostle Paul. The postmark reveals that it comes from the city of Ephesus. After opening the letter I discovered that it was written in Greek rather than English. At the top of the first page was this request: "Please read to your congregation as soon as possible, and then pass on to the other churches."

For several weeks I have worked assiduously with the translation. At times it has been difficult, but now I think I have deciphered its true meaning. May I hasten to say that if in presenting this letter the contents sound strangely Kingian instead of Paulinian, attribute it to my lack of complete objectivity rather than Paul's lack of clarity.

It is miraculous, indeed, that the Apostle Paul should be writing a letter to you and to me nearly 1900 years after his last letter appeared in the New Testament. How this is possible is something of an enigma wrapped in mystery. The important thing, however, is that I can imagine the Apostle Paul writing a letter to American Christians in 1956 A.D. And here is the letter as it stands before me.

I, an apostle of Jesus Christ by the will of God, to you who are in America, Grace be unto you, and peace from God our Father, through our Lord and Savior, Jesus Christ.

For many years I have longed to be able to come to see you. I have heard so much of you and of what you are doing. I have heard of the fascinating and astounding advances that you have made in the scientific realm. I have heard of your dashing subways and flashing airplanes. Through your scientific genius you have been able to dwarf distance and place time in chains. You have been able to carve highways through the stratosphere. So in your world you have made it possible to eat breakfast in New York City and dinner in Paris, France. I have also heard of your skyscraping buildings with their prodigious towers steeping heavenward. I have heard of your great medical advances, which have resulted in the curing of many dread plagues and diseases, and thereby prolonged your lives and made for greater security and physical well-being. All of that is marvelous. You can do so many things in your day that I could not do in the Greco-Roman world of my day. In your age you can travel distances in one day that took me three months to travel. That is wonderful. You have made tremendous strides in the area of scientific and technological development.

But America, as I look at you from afar, I wonder whether your moral and spiritual progress has been commensurate with your scientific progress. It seems to me that your moral progress lags behind your scientific progress. Your poet Thoreau used to talk about "improved means to an unimproved end." How often this is true. You have allowed the material means by which you live to outdistance the spiritual ends for which you live. You have allowed your mentality to outrun your morality. You have allowed your civilization to outdistance your culture. Through your scientific genius you have made of the world a neighborhood, but through your moral and spiritual genius you have failed to make of it a brotherhood. So America, I would urge you to keep your moral advances abreast with your scientific advances.

I am impelled to write you concerning the responsibilities laid upon you to live as Christians in the midst of an un-Christian world. That is what I had to do. That is what every Christian has to do. But I understand that there are many Christians in America who give their ultimate allegiance to manmade systems and customs. They are afraid to be different. Their great concern is to be accepted socially. They live by some such principle as this: "Everybody is doing it, so it must be all right." For so many of you morality is merely group consensus. In your modern sociological lingo, the mores are accepted as the right ways. You have unconsciously come to believe that right is discovered by taking a sort of Gallup poll of the majority opinion. How many are giving their ultimate allegiance to this way.

But American Christians, I must say to you as I said

to the Roman Christians years ago, "Be not conformed to this world, but be ye transformed by the renewing of your mind." Or, as I said to the Philippian Christians, "Ye are a colony of heaven." This means that although you live in the colony of time, your ultimate allegiance is to the empire of eternity. You have a dual citizenry. You live both in time and eternity; both in heaven and earth. Therefore, your ultimate allegiance is not to the government, not to the state, not to nation, not to any manmade institution. The Christian owes his ultimate allegiance to God, and if any earthly institution conflicts with God's will it is your Christian duty to take a stand against it. You must never allow the transitory evanescent demands of manmade institutions to take precedence over the eternal demands of the Almighty God.

I understand that you have an economic system in America known as capitalism. Through this economic system you have been able to do wonders. You have become the richest nation in the world, and you have built up the greatest system of production that history has ever known. All of this is marvelous. But Americans, there is the danger that you will misuse your capitalism. I still contend that money can be the root of all evil. It can cause one to live a life of gross materialism. I am afraid that many among you are more concerned about making a living than making a life. You are prone to judge the success of your profession by the index of your salary and the size of the wheelbase on your automobile, rather than the quality of your service to humanity.

The misuse of capitalism can also lead to tragic exploitation. This has so often happened in your nation. They tell me that one tenth of one percent of the population controls more than forty percent of the wealth. Oh America, how often have you taken necessities from the masses to give luxuries to the classes. If you are to be a truly Christian nation you must solve this problem. You cannot solve the problem by turning to communism, for communism is based on an ethical relativism and a metaphysical materialism that no Christian can accept. You can work within the framework of democracy to bring about a better distribution of wealth. You can use your powerful economic resources to wipe poverty from the face of the earth. God never intended for one group of people to live in superfluous inordinate wealth, while others live in abject deadening poverty. God intends for all of his children to have the basic necessities of life, and he has left in this universe "enough and to spare" for that purpose. So I call upon you to bridge the gulf between abject poverty and superfluous wealth.

I would that I could be with you in person, so that I could say to you face to face what I am forced to say to you in writing. Oh, how I long to share your fellowship.

Let me rush on to say something about the church. Americans, I must remind you, as I have said to so many others, that the church is the Body of Christ. So when the church is true to its nature it knows neither division nor disunity. But I am disturbed about what you are doing to the Body of Christ. They tell me that in America you have within Protestantism more than two hundred and fifty-six denominations. The tragedy is not so much that you have such a multiplicity of denominations, but that most of them are warring against each other with a claim to absolute truth. This narrow sectarianism is destroying the unity of the Body of Christ. You must come to see that God is neither a Baptist nor a Methodist; he is neither a Presbyterian nor an Episcopalian. God is bigger than all of our denominations. If you are to be true witnesses for Christ, you must come to see that, America.

But I must not stop with a criticism of Protestantism. I am disturbed about Roman Catholicism. This church stands before the world with its pomp and power, insisting that it possesses the only truth. It incorporates an arrogance that becomes a dangerous spiritual arrogance. It stands with its noble Pope, who somehow rises to the miraculous heights of infallibility when he speaks *ex cathedra*. But I am disturbed about a person or an institution that claims infallibility in this world. I am disturbed about any church that refuses to cooperate with other churches under the pretense that it is the only true church. I must emphasize the fact that God is not a Roman Catholic, and that the boundless sweep of his revelation cannot be limited to the Vatican. Roman Catholicism must do a great deal to mend its ways.

There is another thing that disturbs me to no end about the American church. You have a white church and you have a Negro church. You have allowed segregation to creep into the doors of the church. How can such a division exist in the true Body of Christ? You must face the tragic fact that when you stand at eleven o'clock on Sunday morning to sing "All Hail the Power of Jesus' Name" and "Dear Lord and Father of All Mankind," you stand in the most segregated hour of Christian America. They tell me that there is more integration in the entertaining world and other secular agencies than there is in the Christian church. How appalling that is.

I understand that there are Christians among you who try to justify segregation on the basis of the Bible. They argue that the Negro is inferior by nature because of Noah's curse upon the children of Ham. Oh my friends, this is blasphemy. This is against everything that the Christian religion stands for. I must say to you as I have said to so many Christians before, that in Christ "there is neither Jew nor Gentile, there is neither bond nor free, there is neither male nor female, for we are all one in Christ Jesus." Moreover, I must reiterate the words that I uttered on Mars Hill: "God that made the world and all things therein . . . hath made of one blood all nations of men for to dwell on all the face of the earth."

So Americans, I must urge you to get rid of every aspect of segregation. The broad universalism standing at the center of the gospel makes both the theory and practice of segregation morally unjustifiable. Segregation is a blatant denial of the unity which we all have in Christ. It substitutes an "I"-"it" relationship for the "I"-"thou" relationship. The segregator relegates the segregated to the status of a thing rather than elevate him to the status of a person. The underlying philosophy of

Christianity is diametrically opposed to the underlying philosophy of segregation, and all the dialectics of the logicians cannot make them lie down together.

I praise your Supreme Court for rendering a great decision just two or three years ago. I am happy to know that so many persons of goodwill have accepted the decision as a great moral victory. But I understand that there are some brothers among you who have risen up in open defiance. I hear that their legislative halls ring loud with such words as "nullification" and "interposition." They have lost the true meaning of democracy and Christianity. So I would urge each of you to plead patiently with your brothers, and tell them that this isn't the way. With understanding goodwill, you are obligated to seek to change their attitudes. Let them know that in standing against integration, they are not only standing against the noble precepts of your democracy, but also against the eternal edicts of God himself. Yes America, there is still the need for an Amos to cry out to the nation: "Let judgment roll down as waters, and righteousness as a mighty stream."

May I say just a word to those of you who are struggling against this evil. Always be sure that you struggle with Christian methods and Christian weapons. Never succumb to the temptation of becoming bitter. As you press on for justice, be sure to move with dignity and discipline, using only the weapon of love. Let no man pull you so low as to hate him. Always avoid violence. If you succumb to the temptation of using violence in your struggle, unborn generations will be the recipients of a long and desolate night of bitterness, and your chief legacy to the future will be an endless reign of meaningless chaos.

In your struggle for justice, let your oppressor know that you are not attempting to defeat or humiliate him, or even to pay him back for injustices that he has heaped upon you. Let him know that you are merely seeking justice for him as well as yourself. Let him know that the festering sore of segregation debilitates the white man as well as the Negro. With this attitude you will be able to keep your struggle on high Christian standards.

Many persons will realize the urgency of seeking to eradicate the evil of segregation. There will be many Negroes who will devote their lives to the cause of freedom. There will be many white persons of goodwill and strong moral sensitivity who will dare to take a stand for justice. Honesty impels me to admit that such a stand will require willingness to suffer and sacrifice. So don't despair if you are condemned and persecuted for righteousness' sake. Whenever you take a stand for truth and justice, you are liable to scorn. Often you will be called an impractical idealist or a dangerous radical. Sometimes it might mean going to jail. If such is the case you must honorably grace the jail with your presence. It might even mean physical death. But if physical death is the price that some must pay to free their children from a permanent life of psychological death, then nothing could be more Christian. Don't worry about persecution, America; you are going to have that if you stand up for a great principle.

I can say this with some authority, because my life was a continual round of persecutions. After my conversion I was rejected by the disciples at Jerusalem. Later I was tried for heresy at Jerusalem. I was jailed at Philippi, beaten at Thessalonica, mobbed at Ephesus, and depressed at Athens. And yet I am still going. I came away from each of these experiences more persuaded than ever before that "neither death nor life, nor angels, nor principalities, nor things present, nor things to come . . . shall separate us from the love of God, which is in Christ Jesus our Lord." I still believe that standing up for the truth of God is the greatest thing in the world. This is the end of life. The end of life is not to be happy. The end of life is not to achieve pleasure and avoid pain. The end of life is to do the will of God, come what may.

I must bring my writing to a close now. Timothy is waiting to deliver this letter, and I must take leave for another church. But just before leaving, I must say to you, as I said to the church at Corinth, that I still believe that love is the most durable power in the world. Over the centuries men have sought to discover the highest good. This has been the chief quest of ethical philosophy. This was one of the big questions of Greek philosophy. The Epicureans and the Stoics sought to answer it; Plato and Aristotle sought to answer it. What is the *summum bonum* of life? I think I have an answer, America. I think I have discovered the highest good. It is love. This principle stands at the center of the cosmos. As John says, "God is love." He who loves is a participant in the being of God. He who hates does not know God.

So American Christians, you may master the intricacies of the English language. You may possess all of the eloquence of articulate speech. But even if you "speak with the tongues of men and angels, and have not love, you are become as sounding brass, or a tinkling cymbal."

You may have the gift of prophecy and understanding [of] all mysteries. You may be able to break into the storehouse of nature and bring out many insights that men never dreamed were there. You may ascend to the heights of academic achievement, so that you will have all knowledge. You may boast of your great institutions of learning and the boundless extent of your degrees. But all of this amounts to absolutely nothing devoid of love.

But even more, Americans, you may give your goods to feed the poor. You may give great gifts to charity. You may tower high in philanthropy. But if you have not love it means nothing. You may even give your body to be burned, and die the death of a martyr. Your spilt blood may be a symbol of honor for generations yet unborn, and thousands may praise you as history's supreme hero. But even so, if you have not love your blood was spilt in vain. You must come to see that it is possible for a man to be self-centered in his self-denial and self-righteous in his self-sacrifice. He may be generous in order to feed his ego and pious in order to feed his pride. Man has the tragic capacity to relegate a heightening virtue to a tragic vice. Without love benevolence becomes egotism, and martyrdom becomes spiritual pride.

So the greatest of all virtues is love. It is here that we find the true meaning of the Christian faith. This is at bottom the meaning of the cross. The great event on Calvary signifies more than a meaningless drama that took place on the stage of history. It is a telescope through which we look out into the long vista of eternity and see the love of God breaking forth into time. It is an eternal reminder to a power-drunk generation that love is [the] most durable power in the world, and that it is at bottom the heartbeat of the moral cosmos. Only through achieving this love can you expect to matriculate into the university of eternal life.

I must say goodbye now. I hope this letter will find you strong in the faith. It is probable that I will not get to see you in America, but I will meet you in God's eternity. And now unto him who is able to keep us from falling, and lift us from the fatigue of despair to the buoyancy of hope, from the midnight of desperation to the daybreak of joy, to him be power and authority, forever and ever. Amen.

DELIVERED AT DEXTER AVENUE BAPTIST CHURCH, MONTGOMERY, ALABAMA, 4 NOVEMBER 1956 [MLKP]

# LOVING YOUR ENEMIES

## INTRODUCTION BY
## REVEREND DR. JOAN BROWN CAMPBELL

y six-year-old granddaughter, Jessica, came home from school last January and excitedly reported to her mother, my daughter Jane, that it was Martin Luther King's birthday. Wide-eyed, she noted that they would be studying this great man. Jane said to her child, "I can help you with that. Your grandmother knew Martin Luther King." With a note of incredulity Jessica said, "No! He's in history." And so he is . . . for a whole generation of young people who know King only through the pages of a history book . . . and yes, they know him through the words and wisdom of his preaching.

But those of us who knew King—those of us who walked with him and those of us who sat at his feet— we all have stories to tell, and he will live on through our stories. Our changed lives continue to bear testimony to his power to love. Martin Luther King had enemies. They were rich and powerful, black and white, male and female, but they were also frightened, small of vision and wed to the status quo. King's enemies wanted to silence his prophetic word. They were desperate to still the marching feet. Those of us who believed in King and who had been transformed by his message wanted him to deal harshly with "the enemy." They were, we told him time and again, dangerous. His bright eyes would cloud up, he would crease his brow and say to us, "Harsh treatment is not the way to deal with those who are dangerous. Violence [he reminded us often] only begets more violence." As he states in the sermon that follows, "The strong person is the person who can cut off the chain of hate, the chain of evil." This was King's most persistent and most difficult message. He would often repeat the words you will find in this sermon: "Somebody must have religion enough and morality enough to cut hate off and inject within the very structure of the universe that strong and powerful element of love."

I was privileged to know and work with Martin Luther King, Jr. His commitment to the beloved community inspired us when he was alive and informs us still. King constantly preached that you must love your enemy. For such a message he was jailed and ridiculed. He was accused of being a perpetrator of violence even as he lived a countercultural life of nonviolence. His very being was a threat to the nation and even to our churches. He was seen as one who disrupted the careful orders of life that preserved privilege and special status. His radical spirituality called the cool, unfeeling faith of many into question. He set about to turn the world upside down, and by his living and his dying he proved that one man armed with truth and courage can move a whole nation. Hear his words:

> Love your enemies that you may be children of your father which is in heaven. We must love our enemies, because only by loving them can we know God and experience the beauty of his holiness. Of course, this is not practical. Life is a matter of getting even, of hitting back, of dog eat dog. Am I saying that Jesus commands us to love those who hurt and oppress us? Do I sound like most preachers—idealistic and impractical? My friends, we have followed the so-called practical way for too long a time now, and it has led inexorably to deeper confusion and chaos. For the salvation of our nation and the salvation of humankind, we must follow another way. This is the only to create the beloved community.

And so, dear Jessica, come to know this man of history. Listen carefully to what he says, for in his message are lessons for living that will guide you all the days of your life.

REVEREND DR. JOAN BROWN CAMPBELL, General Secretary of the National Council of Churches since 1991, is a spiritual leader as well as chief executive officer of the nation's leading ecumenical organization. Under her guidance, the Council works for greater Christian unity and toward justice and peace in the United States and the world. She is the first woman minister to serve as General Secretary of the NCC.

# Loving Your
## Enemies

-⟶⟶⟶⟶⟶⟶-

So I want to turn your attention to this subject: "Loving Your Enemies." It's so basic to me because it is a part of my basic philosophical and theological orientation—the whole idea of love, the whole philosophy of love. In the fifth chapter of the gospel as recorded by Saint Matthew, we read these very arresting words flowing from the lips of our Lord and Master: "Ye have heard that it has been said, 'Thou shall love thy neighbor, and hate thine enemy.' But I say unto you, Love your enemies, bless them that curse you, do good to them that hate you, and pray for them that despitefully use you; that ye may be the children of your Father which is in heaven."

Certainly these are great words, words lifted to cosmic proportions. And over the centuries, many persons have argued that this is an extremely difficult command. Many would go so far as to say that it just isn't possible to move out into the actual practice of this glorious command. They would go on to say that this is just additional proof that Jesus was an impractical idealist who never quite came down to earth. So the arguments abound. But far from being an impractical idealist, Jesus has become the practical realist. The words of this text glitter in our eyes with a new urgency. Far from being the pious injunction of a utopian dreamer, this command is an absolute necessity for the survival of our civilization. Yes, it is love that will save our world and our civilization, love even for enemies.

Now, let me hasten to say that Jesus was very serious when he gave this command; he wasn't playing. He realized that it's hard to love your enemies. He realized that it's difficult to love those persons who seek to defeat you, those persons who say evil things about you. He realized that it was painfully hard, pressingly hard. But he wasn't playing. And we cannot dismiss this passage as just another example of Oriental hyperbole, just a sort of exaggeration to get over the point. This is a basic philosophy of all that we hear coming from the lips of our Master. Because Jesus wasn't playing; because he was serious. We have the Christian and moral responsibility to seek to discover the meaning of these words, and to discover how we can live out this command, and why we should live by this command.

Now, first let us deal with this question, which is the practical question: How do you go about loving your enemies? I think the first thing is this: In order to love your enemies, you must begin by analyzing [your]self. And I'm sure that seems strange to you, that I start out telling you this morning that you love your enemies by beginning with a look at [your]self. It seems to me that that is the first and foremost way to come to an adequate discovery to the how of this situation.

Now, I'm aware of the fact that some people will not like you, not because of something you have done to them, but they just won't like you. I'm quite aware of that. Some people aren't going to like the way you walk; some people aren't going to like the way you talk. Some people aren't going to like you because you can do your job better than they can do theirs. Some people aren't going to like you because other people like you, and because you're popular; and because you're well liked, they aren't going to like you. Some people aren't going to like you because your hair is a little shorter than theirs or your hair is a little longer than theirs. Some people aren't going to like you because your skin is a little brighter than theirs; and others aren't going to like you because your skin is a little darker than theirs. So that some people aren't going to like you. They're going to dislike you, not because of something that you've done to them, but because of various jealous reactions and other reactions that are so prevalent in human nature.

But after looking at these things and admitting these things, we must face the fact that an individual might dislike us because of something that we've done deep down in the past, some personality attribute that we possess, something that we've done deep down in the past and we've forgotten about it; but it was that something that aroused the hate response within the individual. That is why I say, begin with yourself. There might be something within you that arouses the tragic hate response in the other individual.

This is true in our international struggle. We look at the struggle, the ideological struggle between communism on the one hand and democracy on the other, and we see the struggle between America and Russia. Now certainly, we can never give our allegiance to the Russian way of life, to the communistic way of life, because communism is based on an ethical relativism and a metaphysical materialism that no Christian can accept. When we look at the methods of communism, a philosophy where somehow the end justifies the means, we cannot accept that because we believe as Christians that the end is pre-existent in the means. But in spite of all of the weaknesses and evils inherent in communism, we must at the same time see the weaknesses and evils within democracy.

Democracy is the greatest form of government to my mind that man has ever conceived, but the weakness is that we have never touched it. Isn't it true that we have often taken necessities from the masses to give luxuries to the classes? Isn't it true that we have often in our democracy trampled over individuals and races with the iron feet of oppression? Isn't it true that through our Western powers we have perpetuated colonialism and imperialism? And all of these things must be taken under consideration as we look at Russia. We must face the fact that the rhythmic beat of the deep rumblings of discontent from Asia and Africa is at bottom a revolt against the imperialism and colonialism perpetuated by Western civilization all these many years. The success of communism in the world today is due to the failure of democracy to live up to the noble ideals and principles inherent in its system.

And this is what Jesus means when he said: "How is it that you can see the mote in your brother's eye and not see the beam in your own eye?" Or to put it in Moffatt's translation: "How is it that you see the splinter in your brother's eye and fail to see the plank in your own eye?" And this is one of the tragedies of human nature. So we begin to love our enemies and love those persons that hate us whether in collective life or individual life by looking at ourselves.

A second thing that an individual must do in seeking to love his enemy is to discover the element of good in his enemy, and every time you begin to hate that person and think of hating that person, realize that there is some good there and look at those good points which will overbalance the bad points.

I've said to you on many occasions that each of us is something of a schizophrenic personality. We're split up and divided against ourselves. And there is something of a civil war going on within all of our lives. There is a recalcitrant South of our soul revolting against the North of our soul. And there is this continual struggle within the very structure of every individual life. There is something within all of us that causes us to cry out with Ovid, the Latin poet, "I see and approve the better things of life, but the evil things

I do." There is something within all of us that causes us to cry out with Plato that the human personality is like a charioteer with two headstrong horses, each wanting to go in different directions. There is something within each of us that causes us to cry out with Goethe, "There is enough stuff in me to make both a gentleman and a rogue." There is something within each of us that causes us to cry out with Apostle Paul, "I see and approve the better things of life, but the evil things I do."

So somehow the "isness" of our present nature is out of harmony with the eternal "oughtness" that forever confronts us. And this simply means this: That within the best of us, there is some evil, and within the worst of us, there is some good. When we come to see this, we take a different attitude toward individuals. The person who hates you most has some good in him; even the nation that hates you most has some good in it; even the race that hates you most has some good in it. And when you come to the point that you look in the face of every man and see deep down within him what religion calls "the image of God," you begin to love him in spite of—no matter what he does, you see God's image there. There is an element of goodness that he can never slough off. Discover the element of good in your enemy. And as you seek to hate him, find the center of goodness and place your attention there and you will take a new attitude.

Another way that you love your enemy is this: When the opportunity presents itself for you to defeat your enemy, that is the time which you must not do it. There will come a time, in many instances, when the person who hates you most, the person who has misused you most, the person who has gossiped about you most, the person who has spread false rumors about you most, there will come a time when you will have an opportunity to defeat that person. It might be in terms of a recommendation for a job; it might be in terms of helping that person to make some move in life. That's the time you must do it. That is the meaning of love. In the final analysis, love is not this sentimental something that we talk about. It's not merely an emotional something. Love is creative, understanding goodwill for all men. It is the refusal to defeat any individual. When you rise to the level of love, of its great beauty and power, you seek only to defeat evil systems. Individuals who happen to be caught up in that system, you love, but you seek to defeat the system.

The Greek language, as I've said so often before, is very powerful at this point. It comes to our aid beautifully in giving us the real meaning and depth of the whole philosophy of love. And I think it is quite apropos at this point, for you see, the Greek language has three words for love, interestingly enough. It talks about love as *eros*. That's one word for love. *Eros* is a sort of aesthetic love. Plato talks about it a great deal in his dialogues, a sort of yearning of the soul for the realm of the gods. And it's come to us to be a sort of romantic love, though it's a beautiful love. Everybody has experienced *eros* in all of its beauty when you find some individual that is attractive to you and that you pour out all of your like and your love on that individual. That is *eros*, you see, and it's a powerful, beautiful love that is given to us through all of the beauty of literature; we read about it.

Then the Greek language talks about *philia*, and that's another type of love that's also beautiful. It is a sort of intimate affection between personal friends. And this is the type of love that you have for those persons that you're friendly with—your intimate friends, or people that you call on the telephone and you go by to have dinner with, and your roommate in college and that type of thing. It's a sort of reciprocal love. On this level, you like a person because that person likes you. You love on this level, because you are loved. You love on this level, because there's something about the person you love that is likable to you. This too is a beautiful love. You can communicate with a person; you have certain things in common; you like to do things together. This is *philia*.

The Greek language comes out with another word for love. It is the word *agape*. And *agape* is more than *eros; agape* is more than *philia; agape* is something of the understanding, creative, redemptive goodwill for all men. It is a love that seeks nothing in return. It is an overflowing love; it's what theologians would call the love of God working in the lives of men. And when you rise to love on this level, you begin to love men, not because they are likable, but because God loves them. You look at every man, and you love him because you know God loves him. And he might be the worst person you've ever seen.

And this is what Jesus means, I think, in this very passage when he says, "Love your enemy." And it's significant that he does not say, "*Like* your enemy." *Like* is a sentimental something, an affectionate something. There are a lot of people that I find it difficult to like. I don't like what they do to me. I don't like what they say about me and other people. I don't like their attitudes. I don't like some of the things they're doing. I don't like them. But Jesus says love them. And *love* is greater than *like*. *Love* is understanding, redemptive goodwill for all men, so that you love everybody, because God loves them. You refuse to do anything that will defeat an individual, because you have *agape* in your soul. And here you come to the point that you love the individual who does the evil deed while hating the deed that the person does. This is what Jesus means when he says, "Love your enemy." This is the way to do it. When the opportunity presents itself when you can defeat your enemy, you must not do it.

Now, for the few moments left, let us move from the practical how to the theoretical why. It's not only necessary to know how to go about loving your enemies, but also to go down into the question of why we should love our enemies. I think the first reason that we should love our enemies, and I think this was at the very center of Jesus' thinking, is this: that hate for hate only intensifies the existence of hate and evil in the universe. If I hit you and you hit me and I hit you back and you hit me back and go on, you see, that goes on ad infinitum. [*Tapping on pulpit*] It just never ends. Somewhere somebody must have a little sense, and that's the strong person. The strong person is the person who can cut off the chain of hate, the chain of evil. And that is the tragedy of hate, that it doesn't cut it off. It only intensifies the existence of hate and evil in the universe. Somebody must have religion enough and morality enough to cut it off and inject within the very structure of the universe that strong and powerful element of love.

I think I mentioned before that sometime ago my brother and I were driving one evening to Chattanooga, Tennessee, from Atlanta. He was driving the car. And for some reason the drivers were very discourteous that night. They didn't dim their lights; hardly any driver that passed by dimmed his lights. And I remember very vividly, my brother A.D. looked over and in a tone of anger said: "I know what I'm going to do. The next car that comes along here and refuses to dim the lights, I'm going to fail to dim mine and pour them on in all of their power." And I looked at him right quick and said: "Oh no, don't do that. There'd be too much light on this highway, and it will end up in mutual destruction for all. Somebody got to have some sense on this highway."

Somebody must have sense enough to dim the lights, and that is the trouble, isn't it? That as all of the civilizations of the world move up the highway of history, so many civilizations, having looked at other civilizations that refused to dim the lights, and they decided to refuse to dim theirs. And Toynbee tells that out of the twenty-two civilizations that have risen up, all but about seven have found themselves in the junkheap of destruction. It is because civilizations fail to have sense enough to dim the lights. And if somebody doesn't have sense enough to turn on the dim and beautiful and powerful lights of love in this world, the whole of our civilization will be plunged into the abyss of destruction. And we will all end up destroyed because nobody had any sense on the highway of history. Somewhere somebody must have some sense. Men must see that force begets force, hate begets hate, toughness begets toughness. And it is all a descending spiral, ultimately ending in destruction for all and everybody. Somebody must have sense enough and morality enough to cut off the chain of hate and the chain of evil in the universe. And you do that by love.

There's another reason why you should love your enemies, and that is because hate distorts the personality of the hater. We usually think of what hate does for the individual hated or the individuals hated or the groups hated. But it is even more tragic, it is even more ruinous and injurious to the individual who hates. You just begin hating somebody, and you will begin to do irrational things. You can't see straight when you hate. You can't walk straight when you hate. You can't stand upright. Your vision is distorted. There is nothing more tragic than to see an individual whose heart is filled with hate. He comes to the point that he becomes a pathological case. For the person who hates, you can stand up and see a person and that person can be beautiful, and you will call them ugly. For the person who hates, the beautiful becomes ugly and the ugly becomes beautiful. For the person who hates, the good becomes bad and the bad becomes good. For the person who hates, the true becomes false and the false becomes true. That's what hate does. You can't see right. The symbol of objectivity is lost. Hate destroys the very structure of the personality of the hater. And this is why Jesus says hate [does damage to the self] . . . *

. . . The way to be integrated with yourself is be sure that you meet every situation of life with an abounding love. Never hate, because it ends up in tragic, neurotic responses. Psychologists and psychiatrists are telling us today that the more we hate, the more we develop guilt feelings and we begin to subconsciously repress or consciously suppress certain emotions, and they all stack up in our subconscious selves and make for tragic, neurotic responses. And may this not be the neuroses of many individuals as they confront life that that is an element of hate there. And modern psychology is calling on us now to love. But long before modern psychology came into being, the world's greatest psychologist who walked around the hills of Galilee told us to love. He looked at men and said: "Love your enemies; don't hate anybody." It's not enough for us to hate your friends because—to love your friends—be-

---

*Recording interrupted.

cause when you start hating anybody, it destroys the very center of your creative response to life and the universe; so love everybody. Hate at any point is a cancer that gnaws away at the very vital center of your life and your existence. It is like eroding acid that eats away the best and the objective center of your life. So Jesus says love, because hate destroys the hater as well as the hated.

Now there is a final reason I think that Jesus says, "Love your enemies." It is this: that love has within it a redemptive power. And there is a power there that eventually transforms individuals. That's why Jesus says, "Love your enemies." Because if you hate your enemies, you have no way to redeem and to transform your enemies. But if you love your enemies, you will discover that at the very root of love is the power of redemption. You just keep loving people and keep loving them, even though they're mistreating you. Here's the person who is a neighbor, and this person is doing something wrong to you and all of that. Just keep being friendly to that person. Keep loving them. Don't do anything to embarrass them. Just keep loving them, and they can't stand it too long. Oh, they react in many ways in the beginning. They react with bitterness because they're mad because you love them like that. They react with guilt feelings, and sometimes they'll hate you a little more at that transition period, but just keep loving them. And by the power of your love they will break down under the load. That's love, you see. It is redemptive, and this is why Jesus says love. There's something about love that builds up and is creative. There is something about hate that tears down and is destructive. So love your enemies.

I think of one of the best examples of this. We all remember the great president of this United States, Abraham Lincoln—these United States, rather. You remember when Abraham Lincoln was running for president of the United States, there was a man who ran all around the country talking about Lincoln. He said a lot of bad things about Lincoln, a lot of unkind things. And sometimes he would get to the point that he would even talk about his looks, saying, "You don't want a tall, lanky, ignorant man like this as the president of the United States." He went on and on and went around with that type of attitude and wrote about it. Finally, one day Abraham Lincoln was elected president of the United States. And if you read the great biography of Lincoln, if you read the great works about him, you will discover that as every president comes to the point, he came to the point of having to choose a Cabinet. And then came the time for him to choose a secretary of war. He looked across the nation, and decided to choose a man by the name of Mr. Stanton. And when Abraham Lincoln stood around his advisors and mentioned this fact, they said to him: "Mr. Lincoln, are you a fool? Do you know what Mr. Stanton has been saying about you? Do you know what he has done, tried to do to you? Do you know that he has tried to defeat you on every hand? Do you know that, Mr. Lincoln? Did you read all of those derogatory statements that he made about you?" Abraham Lincoln stood before the advisors around him and said: "Oh yes, I know about it; I read about it; I've heard him myself. But after looking over the country, I find that he is the best man for the job."

Mr. Stanton did become secretary of war; and . . . later, Abraham Lincoln was assassinated. And if you go to Washington, you will discover that one of the greatest words or statements ever made about Abraham Lincoln was made about this man Stanton. And as Abraham Lincoln came to the end of his life, Stanton stood up and said: "Now he belongs to the ages." And he made a beautiful statement concerning the character and the stature of this man. If Abraham Lincoln had hated Stanton, if Abraham Lincoln had answered everything Stanton said, Abraham Lincoln would not have transformed and redeemed Stanton. Stanton would have gone to his grave hating Lincoln, and Lincoln would have gone to his grave hating Stanton. But through the power of love Abraham Lincoln was able to redeem Stanton.

That's it. There is a power in love that our world has not discovered yet. Jesus discovered it centuries ago. Mahatma Gandhi of India discovered it a few years ago, but most men and most women never discover it. For they believe in hitting for hitting; they believe in an eye for an eye and a tooth for a tooth; they believe in hating for hating; but Jesus comes to us and says, "This isn't the way."

And oh this morning, as I think of the fact that our

world is in transition now. Our whole world is facing a revolution. Our nation is facing a revolution, our nation. One of the things that concerns me most is that in the midst of the revolution of the world and the midst of the revolution of this nation, that we will discover the meaning of Jesus' words.

History unfortunately leaves some people oppressed and some people oppressors. And there are three ways that individuals who are oppressed can deal with their oppression. One of them is to rise up against their oppressors with physical violence and corroding hatred. But oh, this isn't the way. For the danger and the weakness of this method is its futility. Violence creates many more social problems than it solves. And I've said, in so many instances, that as the Negro, in particular, and colored peoples all over the world struggle for freedom, if they succumb to the temptation of using violence in their struggle, unborn generations will be the recipients of a long and desolate night of bitterness, and our chief legacy to the future will be an endless reign of meaningless chaos. Violence isn't the way.

Another way is to acquiesce and give in, to resign yourself to the oppression. Some people do that. They discover the difficulties of the wilderness moving into the promised land, and they would rather go back to the despots of Egypt because it's difficult to get in the promised land. And so they resign themselves to the fate of oppression; they somehow acquiesce to this thing. But that too isn't the way because noncooperation with evil is as much a moral obligation as is cooperation with good.

But there is another way. And that is to organize mass nonviolent resistance based on the principle of love. It seems to me that this is the only way as our eyes look to the future. As we look out across the years and across the generations, let us develop and move right here. We must discover the power of love, the power, the redemptive power of love. And when we discover that, we will be able to make of this old world a new world. We will be able to make men better. Love is the only way. Jesus discovered that.

Not only did Jesus discover it, even great military leaders discovered that. One day as Napoleon came toward the end of his career and looked back across the years—the great Napoleon that at a very early age had all but conquered the world. He was not stopped until he became, till he moved out to the battle of Leipzig and then to Waterloo. But that same Napoleon one day stood back and looked across the years, and said: "Alexander, Caesar, Charlemagne, and I have built great empires. But upon what did they depend? They depended upon force. But long ago Jesus started an empire that depended on love, and even to this day millions will die for him."

Yes, I can see Jesus walking around the hills and the valleys of Palestine. And I can see him looking out at the Roman Empire with all of her fascinating and intricate military machinery. But in the midst of that, I can hear him saying: "I will not use this method. Neither will I hate the Roman Empire." . . .*

And I'm proud to stand here in Dexter this morning and say that that army is still marching. It grew up from a group of eleven or twelve men to more than seven hundred million today. Because of the power and influence of the personality of this Christ, he was able to split history into A.D. and B.C. Because of his power, he was able to shake the hinges from the gates of the Roman Empire. And all around the world this morning, we can hear the glad echo of heaven ring:

Jesus shall reign wherever sun
Does his successive journeys run;
His kingdom spreads from shore to shore,
Till moon shall wane and wax no more.

We can hear another chorus singing: "All hail the power of Jesus' name!"

We can hear another chorus singing: "Hallelujah, hallelujah! He's King of Kings and Lord of Lords. Hallelujah, hallelujah!"

We can hear another choir singing:

In Christ there is no East or West.
In Him no North or South,
But one great Fellowship of Love
Throughout the whole wide world.

---

*Recording interrupted.

This is the only way.

And our civilization must discover that. Individuals must discover that as they deal with other individuals. There is a little tree planted on a little hill and on that tree hangs the most influential character that ever came in this world. But never feel that that tree is a meaningless drama that took place on the stages of history. Oh no, it is a telescope through which we look out into the long vista of eternity, and see the love of God breaking forth into time. It is an eternal reminder to a power-drunk generation that love is the only way. It is an eternal reminder to a generation depending on nuclear and atomic energy, a generation depending on physical violence, that love is the only creative, redemptive, transforming power in the universe.

So this morning, as I look into your eyes, and into the eyes of all of my brothers in Alabama and all over America and over the world, I say to you, "I love you. I would rather die than hate you." And I'm foolish enough to believe that through the power of this love somewhere, men of the most recalcitrant bent will be transformed. And then we will be in God's kingdom. We will be able to matriculate into the university of eternal life because we had the power to love our enemies, to bless those persons that cursed us, to even decide to be good to those persons who hated us, and we even prayed for those persons who despitefully used us.

Oh God, help us in our lives and in all of our attitudes to work out this controlling force of love, this controlling power that can solve every problem that we confront in all areas. Oh, we talk about politics; we talk about the problems facing our atomic civilization. Grant that all men will come together and discover that as we solve the crisis and solve these problems— the international problems, the problems of atomic energy, the problems of nuclear energy, and yes, even the race problem—let us join together in a great fellowship of love and bow down at the feet of Jesus. Give us this strong determination. In the name and spirit of this Christ, we pray. Amen.

DELIVERED AT DEXTER AVENUE BAPTIST CHURCH, MONTGOMERY, ALABAMA, 17 NOVEMBER 1957 [MLKEC]

# A KNOCK
# AT MIDNIGHT

INTRODUCTION BY REVEREND DR. OTIS MOSS, JR.

t seems providential that I have been invited to comment on Dr. Martin Luther King, Jr.'s, marvelous sermon "A Knock at Midnight." It was a version of this sermon that Dr. King gave in June of 1967 at Mt. Zion Baptist Church in Cincinnati, Ohio, where I was serving as pastor. The occasion was our joint Men's and Women's Day. Eleven months prior to that event, Dr. King officiated at the wedding ceremony for Edwina and me in Atlanta, Georgia, on the Morehouse College campus with the late Dr. Samuel Williams, a former teacher and mentor to Dr. King and my major college professor and mentor.

I must also state that we arranged for the June 1967 worship service to be broadcast on a local radio station, WCIN. The engineer and employee of the station illegally taped the sermon and later made records and sold them across the country. I have not seen or heard from the gentleman since that day. But the illegal, unethical, and fraudulent act is probably indicative of a vast number of unprofessional, unethical, and unauthorized uses of Dr. King's intellectual property that the family has sought to restrain legally.

This sermon, "A Knock at Midnight," addresses the prophetic role of the church in grappling with contemporary problems and challenges.

Dr. King, with keen and sensitive insight, eloquently proclaimed that a profound social and human predicament faced our nation and the world in 1967. He puts his intellect and spiritual insight to work creatively as he points out the blessings and limitations of science and technology in meeting critical human needs. Therefore, it is "midnight within the social order."

It is midnight in the internal life of humankind. "It is also midnight within the moral order."

In this desperate hour of our struggle for meaning, liberation, and salvation, there are persistent knocks on the door of the church. These knocks or appeals are requests for the bread of faith, hope, love, and peace. The relevant question: Will the church feed the weary traveler?

Dr. King finds a hopeful message in the text from Luke 11:5–6. Youths, adults, the neglected, the rejected, the hated, the exploited are all looking for a "little bread to tide them over." In too many instances the church is unresponsive in the face of this "Knock at Midnight." Instead of being a Christ-centered peacemaker and trumpet for justice, the church has too often been a co-partner with war and injustice. Rather than serving as "the conscience of the state," the church in many instances is a servant of the state. Those seeking the bread of economic justice are often disappointed when they knock on the door of the church.

Those who knock at midnight are really "seeking the dawn." Some are seeking the dawn of forgiveness. Many are waiting for the church to "proclaim God's Son, Jesus Christ, to be the hope of men (and women) in all their complex personal and social problems." The church must be the trumpet of dawn in every midnight crisis.

In conclusion, Dr. King gives us an undeniable affirmation of how the dawn broke through when the Montgomery bus protest faced its most threatening and discouraging midnight in November 1956. On November 12 it looked as if the protest would be a failure. But on November 13 came a resounding moral, legal, and historic victory.

This sermon was first delivered by Dr. King approximately ten years before he came to our church in June 1967. Therefore, it was first delivered almost forty years ago, and today it is relevant, rich, powerful, helpful, healing, hopeful, and overflowing with meaning. It is a timely and timeless application of biblical truths found in the ministry of Jesus.

Speaking of the Montgomery struggle, Dr. King says, "The darkest hour of our struggle had become the first hour of victory." We must draw from this faith today as we face anti-affirmative-action movements, Proposition 209, disenfranchising Supreme Court decisions, and redistricting. There is truly "A Knock at Midnight" as we face plant closings and jail construction, public education abandonment, health care crises, a conservative Congress, the re-emergence of states' rights, hate, and fear-driven militias, bloodshed in the Middle East, turmoil in Europe, famine and dislocation in parts of Africa, persecution in China, corruption in Russia. And drugs and violence at home. We must draw strength from the deep reservoir of Dr. King's wisdom. It is midnight, but dawn is coming.

There is "A Knock at Midnight" in every age, in every decade. We can and must respond. The church must respond with manna to match our hunger.

---

REVEREND DR. OTIS MOSS, JR., pastor of Olivet Institutional Baptist Church in Ohio for twenty-two years, is chairman of the Morehouse College Board of Trustees and past chairman of Operation PUSH. His honors include Man of the Year in Religion as well as other civil rights awards, and *Ebony* has twice selected him one of America's greatest preachers. A co-worker and close friend of Dr. Martin Luther King, Jr., Dr. Moss was active in the civil rights movement as an organizer and demonstrator.

# A KNOCK
## AT MIDNIGHT

❖━═◉═━❖

Which of you who has a friend will go to him at
midnight and say to him, "Friend, lend me three
loaves; for a friend of mine has arrived on a journey, and I have nothing to set before him"?

LUKE 11:5–6 (RSV)

Although this parable is
concerned with the power of persistent prayer, it may
also serve as a basis for our thought concerning many
contemporary problems and the role of the church in
grappling with them. It is midnight in the parable; it is
also midnight in our world, and the darkness is so deep
that we can hardly see which way to turn.

It is midnight within the social order. On the international horizon nations are engaged in a colossal and
bitter contest for supremacy. Two world wars have
been fought within a generation, and the clouds of another war are dangerously low. Man now has atomic

and nuclear weapons that could within seconds completely destroy the major cities of the world. Yet the arms race continues and nuclear tests still explode in the atmosphere, with the grim prospect that the very air we breathe will be poisoned by radioactive fallout. Will these circumstances and weapons bring the annihilation of the human race?

When confronted by midnight in the social order we have in the past turned to science for help. And little wonder! On so many occasions science has saved us. When we were in the midnight of physical limitation and material inconvenience, science lifted us to the bright morning of physical and material comfort. When we were in the midnight of crippling ignorance and superstition, science brought us to the daybreak of the free and open mind. When we were in the midnight of dread plagues and diseases, science, through surgery, sanitation, and the wonder drugs, ushered in the bright day of physical health, thereby prolonging our lives and making for greater security and physical well-being. How naturally we turn to science in a day when the problems of the world are so ghastly and ominous.

But alas! science cannot now rescue us, for even the scientist is lost in the terrible midnight of our age. Indeed, science gave us the very instruments that threaten to bring universal suicide. So modern man faces a dreary and frightening midnight in the social order.

This midnight in man's external collective is paralleled by midnight in his internal individual life. It is midnight within the psychological order. Everywhere paralyzing fears harrow people by day and haunt them by night. Deep clouds of anxiety and depression are suspended in our mental skies. More people are emotionally disturbed today than at any other time of human history. The psychopathic wards of our hospitals are crowded, and the most popular psychologists today are the psychoanalysts. Bestsellers in psychology are books such as *Man Against Himself, The Neurotic Personality of Our Times,* and *Modern Man in Search of a Soul.* Bestsellers in religion are such books as *Peace of Mind* and *Peace of Soul.* The popular clergyman preaches soothing sermons on "How to Be Happy" and "How to Relax." Some have been tempted to revise Jesus' command to read, "Go ye into all the world, keep your blood pressure down, and lo, I will make you a well-adjusted personality." All of this is indicative that it is midnight within the inner lives of men and women.

It is also midnight within the moral order. At midnight colors lose their distinctiveness and become a sullen shade of gray. Moral principles have lost their distinctiveness. For modern man, absolute right and wrong are a matter of what the majority is doing. Right and wrong are relative to likes and dislikes and the customs of a particular community. We have unconsciously applied Einstein's theory of relativity, which properly described the physical universe, to the moral and ethical realm.

Midnight is the hour when men desperately seek to obey the eleventh commandment, "Thou shalt not get caught." According to the ethic of midnight, the cardinal sin is to be caught and the cardinal virtue is to get by. It is all right to lie, but one must lie with real finesse. It is all right to steal, if one is so dignified that, if caught, the charge becomes embezzlement, not robbery. It is permissible even to hate, if one so dresses his hating in the garments of love that hating appears to be loving. The Darwinian concept of the survival of the fittest has been substituted by a philosophy of the survival of the slickest. This mentality has brought a tragic breakdown of moral standards, and the midnight of moral degeneration deepens.

As in the parable, so in our world today, the deep darkness of midnight is interrupted by the sound of a knock. On the door of the church millions of people knock. In this country the roll of church members is longer than ever before. More than one hundred and fifteen million people are at least paper members of some church or synagogue. This represents an increase of 100 percent since 1929, although the population has increased by only 31 percent.

Visitors to Soviet Russia, whose official policy is atheistic, report that the churches in that nation not only are crowded, but that attendance continues to grow. Harrison Salisbury, in an article in the *New York Times*, states that Communist officials are disturbed that so many young people express a growing interest in the church and religion. After forty years of the most vigorous efforts to suppress religion, the hierarchy of the Communist party now faces the inescapable fact that millions of people are knocking on the door of the church.

This numerical growth should not be overemphasized. We must not be tempted to confuse spiritual power and large numbers. Jumboism, as someone has called it, is an utterly fallacious standard for measuring positive power. An increase in quantity does not automatically bring an increase in quality. A larger membership does not necessarily represent a correspondingly increased commitment to Christ. Almost always the creative, dedicated minority has made the world better. But although a numerical growth in church membership does not necessarily reflect a concomitant increase in ethical commitment, millions of people do feel that the church provides an answer to the deep confusion that encompasses their lives. It is still the one familiar landmark where the weary traveler by midnight comes. It is the one house which stands where it has always stood, the house to which the man traveling at midnight either comes or refuses to come. Some decide not to come. But the many who come and knock are desperately seeking a little bread to tide them over.

The traveler asks for three loaves of bread. He wants the bread of faith. In a generation of so many colossal disappointments, men have lost faith in God, faith in man, and faith in the future. Many feel as did William Wilberforce, who in 1801 said, "I dare not marry—the future is so unsettled"; or as did William Pitt, who in 1806 said, "There is scarcely anything 'round us but ruin and despair." In the midst of staggering disillusionment, many cry for the bread of faith.

There is also a deep longing for the bread of hope. In the early years of this century many people did not hunger for this bread. The days of the first telephones, automobiles, and airplanes gave them a radiant optimism. They worshiped at the shrine of inevitable progress. They believed that every new scientific achievement lifted man to higher levels of perfection. But then a series of tragic developments, revealing the selfishness and corruption of man, illustrated with frightening clarity the truth of Lord Acton's dictum, "Power tends to corrupt and absolute power corrupts absolutely." This awful discovery led to one of the most colossal breakdowns of optimism in history. For so many people, young and old, the light of hope went out, and they roamed wearily in the dark chambers of pessimism. Many concluded that life has no meaning. Some agreed with the philosopher Schopenhauer that life is an endless pain with a painful end, and that life is a tragicomedy played over and over again with only slight changes in costume and scenery. Others cried out with Shakespeare's Macbeth that life "is a tale told by an idiot, full of sound and fury, signifying nothing." But even in the inevitable moments when all seems hopeless, men know that without hope they cannot really live, and in agonizing desperation they cry for the bread of hope.

And there is the deep longing for the bread of love. Everybody wishes to love and be loved. He who feels that he is not loved feels that he does not count. Much has happened in the modern world to make men feel that they do not belong. Living in a world which has become oppressively impersonal, many of us have come to feel that we are little more than numbers. Ralph Bor-

sodi, in an arresting picture of a world wherein numbers have replaced persons, writes that the modern
mother is often maternity case No. 8434, and her child,
after being fingerprinted and footprinted, becomes No.
8003, and that a funeral in a large city is an event in
Parlor B with Class B flowers and decorations at which
Preacher No. 14 officiates and Musician No. 84 sings
Selection No. 174. Bewildered by this tendency to re-
duce man to a card in a vast index, man desperately
searches for the bread of love.

When the man in the parable knocked on his friend's
door and asked for the three loaves of bread, he received
the impatient retort, "Do not bother me; the door is now
shut, and my children are with me in bed; I cannot get
up and give you anything." How often have men experienced a similar disappointment when at midnight they
knock on the door of the church. Millions of Africans,
patiently knocking on the door of the Christian church
where they seek the bread of social justice, have either
been altogether ignored or told to wait until later, which
almost always means never. Millions of American Negroes, starving for the want of the bread of freedom, have
knocked again and again on the door of so-called white
churches, but they have usually been greeted by a cold indifference or a blatant hypocrisy. Even the white religious
leaders, who have a heartfelt desire to open the door and
provide the bread, are often more cautious than courageous and more prone to follow the expedient than the
ethical path. One of the shameful tragedies of history is
that the very institution which should remove man from

the midnight of racial segregation participates in creating and perpetuating the midnight.

In the terrible midnight of war men have knocked on the door of the church to ask for the bread of peace, but the church has often disappointed them. What more pathetically reveals the irrelevancy of the church in present-day world affairs than its witness regarding war? In a world gone mad with arms buildups, chauvinistic passions, and imperialistic exploitation, the church has either endorsed these activities or remained appallingly silent. During the last two world wars, national churches even functioned as the ready lackeys of the state, sprinkling holy water upon the battleships and joining the mighty armies in singing "Praise the Lord and pass the ammunition." A weary world, pleading desperately for peace, has often found the church morally sanctioning war.

And those who have gone to the church to seek the bread of economic justice have been left in the frustrating midnight of economic privation. In many instances the church has so aligned itself with the privileged classes and so defended the status quo that it has been unwilling to answer the knock at midnight. The Greek church in Russia allied itself with the status quo and became so inextricably bound to the despotic czarist regime that it became impossible to be rid of the corrupt political and social system without being rid of the church. Such is the fate of every ecclesiastical organization that allies itself with things as they are.

The church must be reminded that it is not the master or the servant of the state, but rather the conscience of the state. It must be the guide and the critic of the state, and never its tool. If the church does not recapture its prophetic zeal, it will become an irrelevant social club without moral or spiritual authority. If the church does not participate actively in the struggle for peace and for economic and racial justice, it will forfeit the loyalty of millions and cause men everywhere to say that it has atrophied its will. But if the church will free itself from the shackles of a deadening status quo and, recovering its great historic mission, will speak and act fearlessly and insistently in terms of justice and peace, it will enkindle the imagination of mankind and fire the souls of men, imbuing them with a glowing and ardent love for truth, justice, and peace. Men far and near will know the church as a great fellowship of love that provides light and bread for lonely travelers at midnight.

While speaking of the laxity of the church, I must not overlook the fact that the so-called Negro church has also left men disappointed at midnight. I say "so-called Negro church" because ideally there can be no Negro or white church. It is to their everlasting shame that white Christians developed a system of racial segregation within the church, and inflicted so many indignities upon its Negro worshipers that they had to organize their own churches.

Two types of Negro churches have failed to provide bread. One burns with emotionalism, and the other freezes with classism. The former, reducing worship to entertainment, places more emphasis on volume than on content and confuses spirituality with muscularity. The danger in such a church is that the members may have more religion in their hands and feet than in their hearts and souls. At midnight this type of church has neither the vitality nor the relevant gospel to feed hungry souls.

The other type of Negro church that feeds no midnight traveler has developed a class system and boasts of its dignity, its membership of professional people, and its exclusiveness. In such a church the worship service is cold and meaningless, the music dull and uninspiring, and the sermon little more than a homily on current events. If the pastor says too much about Jesus Christ, the members feel that he is robbing the pulpit of dignity. If the choir sings a Negro spiritual, the members claim an affront to their class status. This type of church tragically fails to recognize that worship at its best is a social experience in which people from all levels of life come together to affirm their oneness and unity under God. At midnight men are altogether ignored because of their limited education, or they are given bread that has been hardened by the winter of morbid class consciousness.

In the parable we notice that after the man's initial disappointment, he continued to knock on his friend's door. Because of his importunity—his persistence—he finally persuaded his friend to open the door. Many men continue to knock on the door of the church at midnight, even after the church has so bitterly disappointed them, because they know the bread of life is there. The church today is challenged to proclaim God's son, Jesus Christ, to be the hope of men in all of their complex personal and social problems. Many will continue to come in quest of answers to life's problems. Many young people who knock on the door are perplexed by the uncertainties of life, confused by daily disappointments, and disillusioned by the ambiguities of history. Some who come have been taken from their schools and careers and cast in the role of soldiers. We must provide them with the fresh bread of hope and imbue them with the conviction that God has the power to bring good out of evil. Some who come are tortured by a nagging guilt resulting from their wandering in the midnight of ethical relativism and their surrender to the doctrine of self-expression. We must lead them to Christ, who will offer them the fresh bread of forgiveness. Some who knock are tormented by the fear of death as they move toward the evening of life. We must provide them with the bread of faith in immortality, so that they may realize that this earthly life is merely an embryonic prelude to a new awakening.

Midnight is a confusing hour when it is difficult to be faithful. The most inspiring word that the church must speak is that no midnight long remains. The weary traveler by midnight who asks for bread is really seeking the dawn. Our eternal message of hope is that dawn will come. Our slave foreparents realized this. They were never unmindful of the fact of midnight, for always there was the rawhide whip of the overseer and the auction block where families were torn asunder to remind them of its reality. When they thought of the agonizing darkness of midnight, they sang:

Oh, nobody knows de trouble I've seen,
Glory Hallelujah!
Sometimes I'm up, sometimes I'm down,
Oh yes, Lord,
Sometimes I'm almost to de groun',
Oh yes, Lord,
Oh, nobody knows de trouble I've seen,
Glory Hallelujah!

Encompassed by a staggering midnight but believing that morning would come, they sang:

I'm so glad trouble don't last alway.
Oh my Lord, oh my Lord, what shall I do?

Their positive belief in the dawn was the growing edge of hope that kept the slaves faithful amid the most barren and tragic circumstances.

Faith in the dawn arises from the faith that God is good and just. When one believes this, he knows that the contradictions of life are neither final nor ultimate. He can walk through the dark night with the radiant conviction that all things work together for good for those that love God. Even the most starless midnight may herald the dawn of some great fulfillment.

At the beginning of the bus boycott in Montgomery, Alabama, we set up a voluntary carpool to get the people to and from their jobs. For eleven long months our carpool functioned extraordinarily well. Then Mayor Gayle introduced a resolution instructing the city's legal department to file such proceedings as it might deem proper to stop the operation of the carpool or any transportation system growing out of the bus boycott. A hearing was set for Tuesday, November 13, 1956.

At our regular weekly mass meeting, scheduled the night before the hearing, I had the responsibility of warning the people that the carpool would probably be enjoined. I knew that they had willingly suffered for nearly twelve months, but could we now ask them to walk back and forth to their jobs? And if not, would we be forced to admit that the protest had failed? For the first time I almost shrank from appearing before them.

When the evening came, I mustered sufficient courage to tell them the truth. I tried, however, to conclude on a note of hope. "We have moved all of these months," I said, "in the daring faith that God is with us in our struggle. The many experiences of days gone by have vindicated that faith in a marvelous way. Tonight we must believe that a way will be made out of no way." Yet I could feel the cold breeze of pessimism pass over the audience. The night was darker than a thousand midnights. The light of hope was about to fade and the lamp of faith to flicker.

A few hours later, before Judge Carter, the city argued that we were operating a "private enterprise" without a franchise. Our lawyers argued brilliantly that the carpool was a voluntary "share-a-ride" plan provided without profit as a service by Negro churches. It became obvious that Judge Carter would rule in favour of the city.

At noon, during a brief recess, I noticed an unusual

commotion in the courtroom. Mayor Gayle was called to the back room. Several reporters moved excitedly in and out of the room. Momentarily a reporter came to the table where, as chief defendant, I sat with the lawyers. "Here is the decision that you have been waiting for," he said. "Read this release."

In anxiety and hope, I read these words: "The United States Supreme Court today unanimously ruled bus segregation unconstitutional in Montgomery, Alabama." My heart throbbed with an inexpressible joy. The darkest hour of our struggle had become the first hour of victory. Someone shouted from the back of the courtroom, "God Almighty has spoken from Washington."

The dawn will come. Disappointment, sorrow, and despair are born at midnight, but morning follows. "Weeping may endure for a night," says the Psalmist, "but joy cometh in the morning." This faith adjourns the assemblies of hopelessness and brings new light into the dark chambers of pessimism.

PUBLISHED IN STRENGTH TO LOVE, 1963

# THE AMERICAN DREAM

INTRODUCTION BY BISHOP T. D. JAKES, SR.

I t would appear to me that in many ways our country has lowered its head into the soft satiny pillow of apathy. We have been lulled to sleep by indifference and rest in the vain pursuit of economical images of success while a stone's throw away there are children dying in the streets. In this generation we question how men can sleep while people die, children starve, and communities collapse. Perhaps it has been good for men to sleep. Perhaps sleep is the only time that prejudice and injustice, indifference and apathy finally recede far enough for conscience to speak and the voice of God to be heard.

"The American Dream" is far more than a sermon. It is a message—no, it is an alarm. It is a trumpet blowing in Zion. It is the shrill cry from the heart of a broken people whose faith will not be denied. As you read through the pages of this manuscript it would be an injustice for you to surmise that what you are reading is the mere meandering of a gifted mind who has assumed the challenge of a sermonic presentation. It is far more than that. All truth is laced with a disturbing undertone. It is meant to disturb the indifferent and ignite the docile, dormant minds of people who choose to look the other way while others die. In this tremendous presentation, Dr. Martin Luther King, Jr., alludes to Independence Day, and as he discusses it, I can but conclude that in reality, independence is not a day, but a journey. A journey whose destination after all these years still lies before us, yet I realize that we are closer to morning than we have ever been before.

The Psalmist David declares that weeping may endure for a night but joy cometh in the morning. It has been a long night. Many have died in the night. Many have fallen prey to the perils of our time. Some lay in the drugged sleep of a decadent generation who have found solace in the arms of narcotics. Some have been deceived. Like children, they close their eyes and play possum, pretending not to see what all the world cannot deny. The truth plain and simple, clear and profound, is indelibly printed upon the pages of this text: that all men—regardless of the color of their skin, the persuasion of their theology, or the level of their intelligence—were created by one God with one blood, designed and fashioned to live on one earth arm and arm, equally suited though diversely sorted.

The greatest biblical events that changed generations and left an indelible impression upon the hearts of men often occur amidst the wilderness and the decadence of life's environment. It was said of John the Baptist that he was a voice crying in the wilderness. He graphically depicts for us the tremendous impact that can be hurled at any people who have had the privilege of listening to a voice from heaven.

Every great revolution, whether it is torn from the pages of biblical history or the *New York Times*, has occurred through the auspices of a man whose mouth was filled with powerful words. My mind ricochets from the fiery preaching of an Elijah whose voice alone summons fire from heaven—to Frederick Douglass, whose blazing eyes and commanding speech created courage in the hearts of men who had been broken by the perils of their plight. I reminisce on the courageous voice of an Esther who faced the King with the tonicity that only comes from being sent by the King of Kings. I reflect on the strong, spirited voice of Rosa Parks, who has become a matriarchal symbol of a tenacious people, fueled by their convictions and empowered by their God. It is after this grand tradition of massive voices that our nation trembled as we heard a brief interlude from a man whose voice carried farther than any microphone could have reached. Dr. Martin Luther King, Jr., introduced a new era and interrupted antiquated concepts of domination and injustice.

It is good for us, at this moment, to hear the melodious sound of his voice rekindled for us through the manuscripts of a man who had the propensity to reach beyond his days and impact generations. The only glimpses of him were the painted images in pictures in the history books at schools that he fought for us to attend. As we reflect upon his memory, we cannot resist the temptation to measure how far we have come and thereby how far we have to go. Thank God for those many people of all colors and classes who have turned his monologue into dialogue and his solo into the harmonious concerto of all enlightened people who recognize that "it is high time for us to wake out of our sleep."

So now let us take a look at the dreamer, and closer still at the dream. It was not his alone, but it is etched in every smeared line and yellow page of the Constitution. It was not his alone. It was a dream sent from God to men who, amidst the darkness of their times, have been blessed with some innate ability to perceive the purpose of God. The American dream may be dreamt at night, but it must be lived in the morning light. So as you read, join me and all men like me. Our likeness has nothing to do with our theology. It has nothing to do with our ethnicity. Our likeness goes back to the first man who was created in the likeness and the image of God. That likeness alone gives all predecessors the liberty to expect freedom, to enjoy equality, and to worship feverishly a God who grants each of us the gift of life and the breath of fresh air. It is not in the spirit of the black race. It is in the spirit of the human race that we say to this nation, "America, it has been a long night, but at last, it's morning!"

Bishop T. D. Jakes, Sr., founded and now serves as pastor of the Potter's House in Dallas. He hosts the TV program *Get Ready*, which is broadcast nationally on Trinity Broadcasting Network (TBN) and Black Entertainment Television (BET), and is the author of fourteen books, including *The Harvest* and *Can You Stand to Be Blessed*.

# THE
# AMERICAN
# DREAM

⊰═◉◉═⊱

I planned to use for the textual basis for our thinking together that passage from the prologue of the book of Job where Satan is pictured as asking God, "Does Job serve thee for nought?" And I'd like to ask you to allow me to hold that sermon [*"Why Serve God?"*] in abeyance and preach it the next time I am in the pulpit in order to share with you some other ideas. This morning I was riding to the airport in Washington, D.C., and on the way to the airport the limousine passed by the Jefferson Monument, and Reverend Andrew Young, my executive assistant, said to me, "It's quite coincidental that we would be passing by the Jefferson Monument on Independence Day." You can get so busy in life that you forget holidays and other days, and it had slipped my mind altogether that today was the Fourth of July. And I said to him, "It is coincidental and quite significant, and I think when I get to Atlanta and go to my pulpit, I will try to preach a sermon in the spirit of the founding fathers of our nation and in the spirit of the Declaration of Independence." And so this morning I would like to use as a subject from which to preach: "The American Dream." (*Yes, sir*)

It wouldn't take us long to discover the substance of that dream. It is found in those majestic words of the Declaration of Independence, words lifted to cosmic proportions: "We hold these truths to be self-evident, that all men are created equal, that they are endowed by [their] Creator with certain inalienable Rights, that among these are Life, Liberty, and the pursuit of Happiness." This is a dream. It's a great dream.

The first saying we notice in this dream is an amazing universalism. It doesn't say "some men," it says "all men." It doesn't say "all white men," it says "all men," which includes black men. It does not say "all Gentiles," it says "all men," which includes Jews. It doesn't say "all Protestants," it says "all men," which includes Catholics. (*Yes, sir*) It doesn't even say "all theists and believers," it says "all men," which includes humanists and agnostics.

Then that dream goes on to say another thing that ultimately distinguishes our nation and our form of government from any totalitarian system in the world. It says that each of us has certain basic rights that are neither derived from or conferred by the state. In order to discover where they came from, it is necessary to move back behind the dim mist of eternity. They are God-given, gifts from his hands. Never before in the history of the world has a sociopolitical document expressed in such profound, eloquent, and unequivocal language the dignity and the worth of human personality. The American dream reminds us, and we should think about it anew on this Independence Day, that every man is an heir of the legacy of dignity and worth.

Now, ever since the founding fathers of our nation dreamed this dream in all of its magnificence—to use a big word that the psychiatrists use—America has been something of a schizophrenic personality, tragically divided against herself. On the one hand we have proudly professed the great principles of democracy, but on the other hand we have sadly practiced the very opposite of those principles.

But now more than ever before, America is challenged to realize its dream, for the shape of the world today does not permit our nation the luxury of an anemic democracy. And the price that America must pay for the continued oppression of the Negro and other minority groups is the price of its own destruction. (*Yes it is*) For the hour is late. And the clock of destiny is ticking out. We must act now before it is too late.

And so it is marvelous and great that we do have a dream, that we have a nation with a dream; and to forever challenge us; to forever give us a sense of urgency; to forever stand in the midst of the "isness" of our terrible injustices; to remind us of the "oughtness" of our noble capacity for justice and love and brotherhood.

This morning I would like to deal with some of the challenges that we face today in our nation as a result of the American dream. First, I want to reiterate the fact that we are challenged more than ever before to respect the dignity and the worth of all human personality. We are challenged to really believe that all men are created

equal. And don't misunderstand that. It does not mean
that all men are created equal in terms of native endowment, in terms of intellectual capacity—it doesn't mean
that. There are certain bright stars in the human firma-
ment in every field. (*Yes, sir*) It doesn't mean that every
musician is equal to a Beethoven or Handel, a Verdi or a
Mozart. It doesn't mean that every physicist is equal to an
Einstein. It does not mean that every literary figure in
history is equal to Aeschylus and Euripides, Shakespeare
and Chaucer. (*Make it plain*) It does not mean that every
philosopher is equal to Plato, Aristotle, Immanuel Kant,
and Friedrich Hegel. It doesn't mean that. There are individuals who do excel and rise to the heights of genius
in their areas and in their fields. What it does mean is
that all men are equal in intrinsic worth. (*Yes*)

You see, the founding fathers were really influenced
by the Bible. The whole concept of the *imago dei*, as it
is expressed in Latin, the "image of God," is the idea
that all men have something within them that God in-
jected. Not that they have substantial unity with God,
but that every man has a capacity to have fellowship
with God. And this gives him a uniqueness, it gives
him worth, it gives him dignity. And we must never
forget this as a nation: There are no gradations in the
image of God. Every man from a treble white to a bass
black is significant on God's keyboard, precisely because every man is made in the image of God. One day
we will learn that. (*Yes*) We will know one day that
God made us to live together as brothers and to respect
the dignity and worth of every man.

This is why we must fight segregation with all of our nonviolent might. (*Yes, sir. Make it plain*) Segregation is not only inconvenient—that isn't what makes it wrong. Segregation is not only sociologically untenable—that isn't what makes it wrong. Segregation is not only politically and economically unsound—that is not what makes it wrong. Ultimately, segregation is morally wrong and sinful. To use the words of a great Jewish philosopher that died a few days ago, Martin Buber, "It's wrong because it substitutes an 'I'-'it' relationship for the 'I'-'thou' relationship and relegates persons to the status of things." That's it. (*Yes, sir*)

I remember when Mrs. King and I were in India, we journeyed down one afternoon to the southernmost part of India, the state of Kerala, the city of Trivandrum. That afternoon I was to speak in one of the schools, what we would call high schools in our country, and it was a school attended by and large by students who were the children of former untouchables. Now, you know in India, there was the caste system—and India has done a marvelous job in grappling with this problem—but you had your full caste and individuals were in one of the castes. And then you had some sixty or seventy million people who were considered outcasts. They were the untouchables; they could not go places that other people went; they could not do certain things. And this was one of the things that Mahatma Gandhi battled—along with his struggle to end the long night of colonialism—also to end the long night of the caste system and caste untouchability. You remember some of his great fasts were around the question of making equality a reality for the Harijans, as they were called, the "untouchables." He called them the children of God, and he even adopted an untouchable as his daughter. He demonstrated in his own personal life and in his family that he was going to revolt against a whole idea. And I remember that afternoon when I stood up in that school. The principal introduced me and then as he came to the conclusion of his introduction, he says, "Young people, I would like to present to you a fellow untouchable from the United States of America." And for the moment I was a bit shocked and peeved that I would be referred to as an untouchable. (*Glory to God*)

Pretty soon my mind dashed back across the mighty Atlantic. And I started thinking about the fact that at that time no matter how much I needed to rest my tired body after a long night of travel, I couldn't stop in the average motel of the highways and the hotels of the cities of the South. I started thinking about the fact that no matter how long an old Negro woman had been shopping downtown and got a little tired and needed to get a hamburger or a cup of coffee at a lunch counter, she couldn't get it there. (*Preach*) I started thinking about the fact that still in too many instances, Negroes have to go to the back of the bus and have to stand up over empty seats. (*Yes, sir*) I started thinking about the fact that my children and the other children that would be born would have to go to segregated schools. I started thinking about the fact: twenty million of my brothers and sisters were still smothering in an airtight cage of poverty in an affluent society. I started thinking about the fact: (*Make it plain*) These twenty million brothers and sisters were still by and large housed in rat-infested, unendurable slums in the big cities of our nation, still attended inadequate schools faced with improper recreational facilities. And I said to myself, "Yes, I am an untouchable, and every Negro in the United States of America is an untouchable." And this is the evilness of segregation: It stigmatizes the segregated as an untouchable in a caste system. We hold these truths to be self-evident, if we are to be a great nation, that all men (*All men*) are created equal. God's black children are as significant as his white children. (*Yes, sir*) "We hold these truths to be self-evident." One day we will learn this.

The other day Mrs. King and I spent about ten days down in Jamaica. I'd gone down to deliver the commencement address at the University of the West Indies. I always love to go to that great island, which I consider the most beautiful island in all the world. The government prevailed upon us to be their guests and spend some time and try to get a little rest while there on the speaking tour. And so for those days we traveled all over Jamaica. And over and over again I was impressed by one thing. Here you have people from many national backgrounds: Chinese, Indians, so-called Negroes, and you can just go down the line, Europeans, and people from many, many nations. Do you know they all live there and they have a motto in Jamaica, "Out of many people, one people." And they say, "Here in Jamaica we are not Chinese, (*Make it plain*) we are not Japanese, we are not Indians, we are not Negroes, we are not Englishmen, we are not Canadians. But we are all one big family of Jamaicans." One day, here in America, I hope that we will see this and we will become one big family of Americans. Not white Americans, not black Americans, not Jewish or Gentile Americans, not Irish or Italian Americans, not Mexican Americans, not Puerto Rican Americans, but just Americans. One big family of Americans.

And I tell you this morning, my friends, the reason we got to solve this problem here in America: because God somehow called America to do a special job for mankind and the world. (*Yes, sir. Make it plain*) Never before in the history of the world have so many racial groups and so many national backgrounds assembled together in one nation. And somehow, if we can't solve the problem in America the world can't solve the problem, because America is the world in miniature and the world is America writ large. And God set us out with all of the opportunities. (*Make it plain*) He set us between two great oceans; (*Yes, sir*) made it possible for us to live with some of the great natural resources of the world. And there he gave us through the minds of our forefathers a great creed: "We hold these truths to be self-evident, that all men (*Yes, sir*) are created equal."

Now, that doesn't only apply on the race issue, it applies on the class question. You know, sometimes a class system can be as vicious and evil as a system based on racial injustice. (*Yes, sir*) When we say, "We hold these truths to be self-evident, that all men are created

equal," and when we live it out, we know as I say so
often that the "no D." is as significant as the "Ph.D."
And the man who has been to "No House" is as significant as the man who's been to Morehouse. (*Make
it plain today*) We build our little class systems, and you
know you got a lot of Negroes with classism in their
veins. (*Sure*) You know that they don't want to be
bothered with certain other Negroes and they try to
separate themselves from them. (*Amen*)

I remember when I was in theological school, and we
were coming to the end of our years there, a classmate—he came to me to talk with me—said that he
wanted to invite his mother up. And she'd struggled in
order to help him get through school. He wanted to invite his mother up, but he said, "You know, the problem is I don't know if she would quite fit in this
atmosphere. You know, her verbs aren't quite right; and
she doesn't know how to dress too well; she lives in a
rural area." And I wanted to say to him so bad that you
aren't fit to finish this school. (*Yes*) If you cannot acknowledge your mother, if you cannot acknowledge
your brothers and sisters, even if they have not risen to
the heights of educational attainment, then you aren't
fit (*Have mercy*) to go out and try to preach to men and
women. (*Amen*)

Oh, I'll tell you this morning, and you learn this and
you discover the meaning of "God's image." You'll
know what the New Testament means when it says
that "I revealed it to babes and so often withheld it
from the wise." And I have learned a great deal in my

few years, not only from the philosophers that I have studied with in the universities, not only from the theologians and the psychologists and the historians, but so often from that humble human being who didn't have the opportunity to get an education but who had something basic deep down within. (*Yes*) Sometimes Aunt Jane on her knees can get more truth than the philosopher on his tiptoes. (*Yes. Amen*) And this is what "all men are made in the image of God" tells us. We must believe this and we must live by it. (*Yes*)

This is why we must join the war against poverty (*Yes, sir*) and believe in the dignity of all work. What makes a job menial? I'm tired of this stuff about menial labor. What makes it menial is that we don't pay folk anything. (*Yes, sir*) Give somebody a job and pay them some money so they can live and educate their children and buy a home and have the basic necessities of life. And no matter what the job is, it takes on dignity.

I submit to you when I took off on that plane this morning, I saw men go out there in their overalls. (*Yes, sir. Every time*) I saw them working on things here and there, and saw some more going out there to put the breakfast on there so that we could eat on our way to Atlanta. (*Make it plain*) And I said to myself that these people who constitute the ground crew are just as significant as the pilot, because this plane couldn't move if you didn't have the ground crew. (*Amen*) I submit to you that in Hugh Spaulding or Grady Hospital, (*Preach it*) the woman or the man who goes in there to sweep the floor is just as significant as the doctor, (*Yes*) because

if he doesn't get that dust off the floor germs will begin
to circulate. And those same germs can do injury and
harm to the human being. I submit to you this morning (*Yes*) that there is dignity in all work (*Have mercy*)
when we learn to pay people decent wages. Whoever
cooks in your house, whoever sweeps the floor in your
house is just as significant as anybody who lives in that
house. (*Amen*) And everybody that we call a maid is
serving God in a significant way. (*Preach it*) And I love
the maids, I love the people who have been ignored,
and I want to see them get the kind of wages that they
need. And their job is no longer a menial job, (*No, sir*)
for you come to see its worth and its dignity.

Are we really taking this thing seriously? "All men are
created equal." (*Amen*) And that means that every man
who lives in a slum today (*Preach it*) is just as significant
as John D., Nelson, or any other Rockefeller. Every man
who lives in the slum is just as significant as Henry Ford.
All men are created equal, and they are endowed by their
Creator with certain inalienable rights, rights that can't
be separated from you. [*Clap*] Go down and tell them,
(*No*) "You may take my life, but you can't take my right
to life. You may take liberty from me, but you can't take
my right to liberty. You may take from me the desire, you
may take from me the propensity to pursue happiness,
but you can't take from me my right to pursue happiness." (*Yes*) "We hold these truths to be self-evident, that
all men are created equal and endowed by their Creator
with certain inalienable Rights and among these are Life,
Liberty, and the pursuit of Happiness." (*Yes, sir*)

Now, there's another thing that we must never forget. If we are going to make the American dream a reality, (*Yes*) we are challenged to work in an action program to get rid of the last vestiges of segregation and discrimination. This problem isn't going to solve itself, however much people tell us this. However much the Uncle Toms and Nervous Nellies in the Negro communities tell us this, this problem isn't just going to work itself out. (*No, sir*) History is the long story of the fact (*Yes*) that privileged groups seldom give up their privileges without strong resistance, and they seldom do it voluntarily. And so if the American dream is to be a reality, we must work to make it a reality and realize the urgency of the moment. And we must say, now is the time to make real the promises of democracy. Now is the time to get rid of segregation and discrimination. Now is the time to make Georgia a better state. Now is the time to make the United States a better nation. (*Yes*) We must live with that, and we must believe that.

And I would like to say to you this morning what I've tried to say all over this nation, what I believe firmly: that in seeking to make the dream a reality we must use and adopt a proper method. I'm more convinced than ever before that nonviolence is the way. I'm more convinced than ever before that violence is impractical as well as immoral. If we are to build right here a better America, we have a method (*Yes, sir*) as old as the insights of Jesus of Nazareth and as modern as the techniques of Mohandas K. Gandhi. We need not hate; we need not use violence. We can stand up before our most violent opponent and say: We will match your capacity to inflict suffering by our capacity to endure suffering. We will meet your physical force with soul force. (*Make it plain*) Do to us what you will and we will still love you. We cannot in all good conscience obey your unjust laws, because noncooperation with evil is as much a moral obligation as is cooperation with good, and so throw us in jail. (*Make it plain*) We will go in those jails and transform them from dungeons of shame to havens of freedom and human dignity. Send your hooded perpetrators of violence into our communities after midnight hours and drag us out on some wayside road and beat us and leave us half-dead, and as difficult as it is, we will still love you. (*Amen*) Somehow go around the country and use your propaganda agents to make it appear that we are not fit culturally, morally, or otherwise for integration, and we will still love you. (*Yes*) Threaten our children and bomb our homes, and as difficult as it is, we will still love you. (*Yeah*)

But be assured that we will ride you down by our capacity to suffer. One day we will win our freedom, but we will not only win freedom for ourselves, we will so appeal to your heart and your conscience that we will win you in the process. And our victory will be a double victory.

Oh yes, love is the way. (*Yes*) Love is the only absolute. More and more I see this. I've seen too much hate to want to hate myself; hate is too great a burden to bear. (*You bet. Yes*) I've seen it on the faces of too many sheriffs of the South—I've seen hate. In the faces and even the walk of too many Klansmen of the South, I've seen hate. Hate distorts the personality. Hate does something to the soul that causes one to lose his objectivity. The man who hates can't think straight; (*Amen*) the man who hates can't reason right; the man who hates can't see right; the man who hates can't walk right. (*Yeah*) And I know now that Jesus is right, (*Yeah*) that love is the way. And this is why John said, "God is love," (*Yes, sir*) so that he who hates does not know God, but he who loves (*Get in the door*) at that moment has the key that opens the door (*Yeah*) to the meaning of ultimate reality. So this morning there is so much that we have to offer to the world. (*Yes, sir*)

We have a great dream. (*Great dream*) It started way back in 1776, and God grant that America will be true to her dream.

About two years ago now, I stood with many of you who stood there in person and all of you who were there in spirit before the Lincoln Monument in Washington. (*Yes*) As I came to the end of my speech there, I tried to tell the nation about a dream I had. I must confess to you this morning that since that sweltering August afternoon in 1963, my dream has often turned into a nightmare. (*Lord*) I've seen it shattered. I saw it shattered one night on Highway 80 in Alabama when Mrs. Viola Liuzzo was shot down. (*Lord, Lord*) I had a nightmare and saw my dream shattered one night in Marion, Alabama, when Jimmie Lee Jackson was shot down. (*Lord*) I saw my dream shattered one night in Selma when Reverend Reeb was clubbed to the ground by a vicious racist and later died. And oh, I continue to see it shattered as I walk through the Harlems of our nation (*Yes*) and see sometimes ten and fifteen Negroes trying to live in one or two rooms. (*Yes*) I've been down to the Delta of Mississippi since then, and I've seen my dream shattered as I met hundreds of people who didn't earn more than six or seven dollars a week. I've seen my dream shattered as I've walked the streets of Chicago (*Make it plain*) and seen Negroes, young men and women, with a sense of utter hopelessness because they can't find any jobs. And they see life as a long and desolate corridor with no exit signs. And not only Negroes at this point. I've seen my dream shattered because I've been through Appalachia, and I've seen my white brothers along with Negroes living in poverty. (*Yeah*) And I'm concerned about white poverty as much as I'm concerned about Negro poverty. (*Make it plain*)

So yes, the dream has been shattered, (*Amen*) and I have had my nightmarish experiences, but I tell you this morning once more that I haven't lost the faith. (*No, sir*) I still have a dream (*A dream. Yes, sir*) that one day all of God's children will have food and clothing and material well-being for their bodies, culture and education for their minds, and freedom for their spirits. (*Yes*)

I still have a dream this morning: (*Yes*) One day all of God's black children will be respected like his white children.

I still have a dream this morning (*Yes*) that one day the lion and the lamb will lie down together, and every man will sit under his own vine and fig tree and none shall be afraid.

I still have a dream this morning that one day all men everywhere will recognize that out of one blood God made all men to dwell upon the face of the earth.

I still have a dream this morning (*Yes, sir*) that one day every valley shall be exalted, and every mountain and hill will be made low; the rough places will be made plain, and the crooked places straight; and the glory of the Lord shall be revealed, and all flesh shall see it together.

I still have a dream this morning (*Amen*) that truth will reign supreme and all of God's children will respect the dignity and worth of human personality. And when this day comes the morning stars will sing together (*Yes*) and the sons of God will shout for joy.

"We hold these truths to be self-evident, that all men (*All right*) are created equal, that they are endowed by their Creator with certain inalienable Rights, (*Yes, sir*) that among these are Life, Liberty, and the pursuit of Happiness."

We open the doors of the church now. If someone needs to accept Christ, (*Yes, sir*) this is a marvelous opportunity, a great moment to make a decision. And as we sing together, we bid you come at this time by Christian experience, baptism, watch care. But come at this moment, become a part of this great Christian fellowship, and accept Christ (*Yes, sir*) as your personal savior.

DELIVERED AT EBENEZER BAPTIST CHURCH, ATLANTA, GEORGIA, 4 JULY 1965 [MLKEC]

# GUIDELINES FOR A CONSTRUCTIVE CHURCH

## INTRODUCTION BY REVEREND FLOYD H. FLAKE

artin Luther King, Jr., had the ability to take contemporary issues and interpret them in a theological context challenging people to examine their roles as Christians or as members of other denominations that profess to practice goodwill toward all humanity. He made the words of the prophets of the Old Testament and Jesus of the New Testament relevant to the poor that he advocated, the brokenhearted to whom he preached messages of wholeness, those held captive by historical prejudices, persons who were blind to the prospects of an integrated society, and the many "Negroes" who, although they were legally emancipated, were still victims of a system that condoned overt racism and unfair practices toward them.

In "Guidelines for a Constructive Church," Martin Luther King, Jr., begins by addressing the problem of school segregation that the Supreme Court declared unconstitutional in 1954. He notes that the court's mandate was for integration to move forward "with deliberate speed"; but by 1966 the process had been slowed to a crawl. Dr. King recalls the turning point came when the Department of Education issued guidelines to every school district directing them to integrate or else lose federal funds.

Using Isaiah 61 as his text, he eloquently unveils the "Guidelines for a Constructive Church" that must be followed if the church doesn't want "the funds of grace cut off from the divine treasury." He challenges the church to respond to the human brokenheartedness that invades the life of every human being at some point or another. Second, he calls the church to be true to its mission of fighting racial injustice despite fear of reprisal. He further iterates that in order to follow these guidelines, those in church leadership must be bold enough to proclaim the message of freedom and liberation. Finally, Dr. King announces that "the acceptable year of the Lord" is now.

The failure of the public school system is one of the most glaring problems facing society today. Therefore, the church needs to reexamine itself in relationship to Dr. King's guidelines. I believe that this is the acceptable year to offer options of education to poor children who are stuck in a system that is not preparing them to compete in today's global society. This is the acceptable year to bring relief to the brokenhearted parents who see their children move through the school system by social promotion and come to the end of the process as functional—and in many cases, dysfunctional—illiterates. This is the acceptable year of the Lord to boldly challenge the last vestiges of segregation by gender, class, and race.

---

THE REVEREND CONGRESSMAN FLOYD H. FLAKE recently retired after eleven years' service in the House of Representatives (Dem.-NY) to return full-time as pastor of the Allen African Methodist Episcopal Church in Jamaica, New York, where he has served since 1976. The Allen Ministries include a Christian school, a social services center with a city-funded walk-in clinic, a senior citizens' housing complex, and a strip of shopping centers.

# GUIDELINES FOR
# A CONSTRUCTIVE
# CHURCH

This morning I would like to submit to you that we who are followers of Jesus Christ, and we who must keep his church going and keep it alive, also have certain basic guidelines to follow. Somewhere behind the dim mist of eternity, God set forth his guidelines. And through his prophets, and above all through his son Jesus Christ, he said that "there are some things that my church must do. There are some guidelines that my church must follow." And if we in the church don't want the funds of grace cut off from the divine treasury, we've got to follow the guidelines. (*That's right*) The guidelines are clearly set forth for us in some words uttered by our Lord and Master as he went in the temple one day, and he went back to Isaiah and quoted from him. And he said, "The Spirit of the Lord is upon me, because he hath anointed me (*Yes, sir*) to preach the gospel to the poor, (*Yes, sir*) he hath sent me to heal the brokenhearted, to preach deliverance to the captives, and recovering of sight to the blind, (*Yes*) to set at liberty them that are bruised, to preach the acceptable year of the Lord." These are the guidelines.

You see, the church is not a social club, although some people think it is. (*Make it plain*) They get caught up in their exclusivism, and they feel that it's a kind of social club with a thin veneer of religiosity, but the church is not a social club. (*Make it plain*) The church is not an entertainment center, although some people think it is. You can tell in many churches how they act in church, which demonstrates that they think it's an entertainment center. The church is not an entertainment center. Monkeys are to entertain, not preachers.

But in the final analysis the church has a purpose. The church is dealing with man's ultimate concern. And therefore it has certain guidelines that it must follow.

Now, I wish time permitted me to go into every aspect of this text, but I want to just mention a few. Let us first think of the fact that if the church is following its guidelines, it seeks to heal (*Yes, sir*) the brokenhearted. Now, there is probably no human condition more tantalizing than a broken heart. You see, brokenheartedness is not a physical condition; it's a condition of spiritual exhaustion. And who here this morning has not experienced a broken heart? I would say brokenheartedness comes basically from the trying experience of disappointment. And I don't believe there are many people here this morning under the sound of my voice who have not been disappointed about something. (*Yes. That's right*)

Here is a young man or a young woman dreaming of some great career and setting out in school to try to make that career possible, only to discover that they don't quite have the mental faculties, the technical know-how, to achieve excellence in that particular field. And so they end up having to choose life's second best, and because of this they end up with a broken heart. (*Make it plain*)

Here is a couple standing before the altar in a marriage that seems to be born in heaven, only to discover that six months or a year later the conflicts and the dissensions begin to develop; arguments and misunderstandings begin to unfold. (*Yes, sir*) And that same marriage which a year earlier seemed to have been born in heaven ends up in the divorce court, (*Yes*) and the individuals are left with a broken heart.

Here is a family, (*Make it plain*) a mother and father striving desperately to train their children up in the way that they should go. Working hard to make their education possible; working hard to give them a sense of direction, praying fervently for their guidance. And yet, in spite of all of this, one or two of the children end up taking the wrong road, (*Yes*) moving toward some strange and tragic far country. And the parents end up having to acknowledge that the children that they raised are prodigals lost in a far country, and they end up with a broken heart.

And then there comes life's ultimate tragedy, that

*something* that always makes for a broken heart. Who this morning hasn't experienced it? When you must stand before the bier of a loved one. (*Yes, sir*) That day when the casket rolls down the aisle. That experience called death, which is the irreducible common denominator of all men. And no one can lose a loved one, no one can lose a mother or father, sister, brother, a child, without ending up with a broken heart. Brokenheartedness is a reality in life.

And Sunday after Sunday, week after week, people come to God's church with broken hearts. (*Yes, sir*) They need a word of hope. And the church has an answer—if it doesn't, it isn't a church. (*Yes*) The church must say in substance that brokenheartedness is a fact of life. Don't try to escape when you come to that experience. Don't try to repress it. Don't end up in cynicism. Don't get mean when you come to that experience. (*Make it plain*) The church must say to men and woman that Good Friday (*Yes, sir*) is a fact of life. The church must say to people that failure is a fact of life. Some people are only conditioned to success. They are only conditioned to fulfillment. Then when the trials and the burdens of life unfold, they can't stand up with it. But the church must tell men (*Yes, sir*) that Good Friday's as much a fact of life as Easter; failure is as much a fact of life as success; disappointment is as much a fact of life as fulfillment. And the church must tell men to take your burden, (*Yes, sir*) take your grief and look at it, don't run from it. Say that this is my grief (*Yes, sir*) and I must bear it. (*Yes*) Look at it hard enough and say, "How can I transform this liability into an asset?" (*Yes*)

This is the power that God gives you. He doesn't say that you're going to escape tension; he doesn't say that you're going to escape disappointment; he doesn't say that you're going to escape trials and tribulations. But what religion does say is this: that if you have faith in God, (*Yes*) that God has the power (*Yes, sir*) to give you a kind of inner equilibrium through your pain. So let not your heart be troubled. (*No, sir*) "If ye believe in God, ye believe also in me." Another voice rings out, "Come unto me, all ye that labor (*Yes, sir. Yes*) and are heavy laden." As if to say, "Come unto me, all ye that are burdened down. Come unto me, all ye that are frustrated. Come unto me, all ye with clouds of anxiety floating in your mental skies. Come unto me, all ye that are broke down. (*Yes, sir*) Come unto me, all ye that are heartbroken. (*Yes*) Come unto me, all ye that are laden with heavy ladens, and I will give you rest." And the rest that God gives (*Yes*) is the rest that passeth all understanding. (*Yes it does*) The world doesn't understand that kind of rest, because it's a rest that makes it possible (*Yes*) for you to stand up amid outer storms, and yet you maintain inner calm. (*Yes*) If the church is true to its guidelines, (*Yes*) it heals the brokenhearted.

Secondly, when the church is true to its guidelines, it sets out to preach deliverance (*Yes, sir*) to them that are captive. (*Yes, sir*) This is the role of the church: to free people. This merely means to free those who are slaves. Now, if you notice some churches, they never read this part. Some churches aren't concerned about freeing anybody. Some white churches (*Make it plain*) face the fact Sunday after Sunday that their members are slaves to prejudice, (*Yes, sir*) slaves to fear. You got a third of them, or a half of them or more, slaves to their prejudices. (*Yes, sir*) And the preacher does nothing to free them from their prejudice so often. (*Make it plain. Yes*) Then you have another group sitting up there who would really like to do something about racial injustice, but they are afraid of social, political, and economic reprisals, (*Make it plain*) so they end up silent. And the preacher never says anything to lift their souls and free them from that fear. (*Make it plain*) And so they end up captive. You know this often happens in the Negro church. (*Yeah*) You know, there are some Negro preachers that have never opened their mouths about the freedom movement. And not only have they not opened their mouths, they haven't done anything about it. And every now and then you get a few members: (*Make it plain*) "They talk too much about civil rights in that church." (*That's right*) I was talking with a preacher the other day and he said a few of his members were saying that. I said, "Don't pay any attention to them. (*Make it plain*) Because number one, the members didn't anoint you to preach. (*Yeah*) And any preacher who allows members to tell him what to preach isn't much of a preacher." (*Amen*)

For the guidelines made it very clear that God anointed. (*Yes, sir*) No member of Ebenezer Baptist Church called me to the ministry. (*No, sir*) You called me to Ebenezer, and you may turn me out of here, but you can't turn me out of the ministry, because I got my guidelines and my anointment from God Almighty. And *anything* I want to say, I'm going to say it from this pulpit. (*Make it plain*) It may hurt somebody, I don't know about that; somebody may not agree with it. (*Tell them*) But when God speaks, who can but prophesy? (*Amen*) The word of God is upon me like *fire* shut up in my bones, (*Yes. That's right*) and when God's word gets upon me, I've got to say it, I've got to tell it all over everywhere. [*Shouting*] (*Yes*) And God has called me (*Yes*) to deliver those that are in captivity. (*Yes, sir*)

Some people are suffering. (*Make it plain*) Some people are hungry this morning. (*Yes*) [*Clap*] Some people are still living with segregation and discrimination this morning. (*Yes, sir*) I'm going to preach about it. (*Preach it. I'm with you*) I'm going to fight for them. I'll die for them if necessary, because I got my guidelines clear. (*Yes*) And the God that I serve and the God that called me to preach (*Yes. Amen*) told me that every now and then I'll have to go to jail for them. (*Make it plain*) Every now and then I'll have to agonize and suffer for the freedom of his children. (*Yes*) I even may have to die for it. But if that's necessary, I'd rather follow the guidelines of God (*Yes*) than to follow the guidelines of men. (*Yes*) The church is called to set free (*Yes*) those that are captive, (*Yes, sir*) to set free those that are victims of the slavery of segregation and discrimination, those who are caught up in the slavery of fear and prejudice. (*Make it plain*)

And then the church, if it is true to its guidelines, must preach the acceptable year of the Lord. (*Yes, sir. Make it plain*) You know the acceptable year of the Lord is the year that is acceptable to God because it fulfills the demands of his kingdom. Some people reading this passage feel that it's talking about some period beyond history, (*Make it plain*) but I say to you this morning that the acceptable year of the Lord can be this year. (*Yes*) And the church is called to preach it.

The acceptable year of the Lord is any year (*Amen*) when men decide to do right.

The acceptable year of the Lord is any year when men will stop lying and cheating. (*Amen. Make it plain*)

The acceptable year of the Lord is that year when women will start using the telephone for constructive purposes (*Yes*) and not to spread malicious gossip and false rumors on their neighbors. (*Right*)

The acceptable year of the Lord is any year (*Any year*) when men will stop throwing away the precious lives that God has given them in riotous living. (*Make it plain*)

The acceptable year of the Lord (*Yes*) is that year when people in Alabama (*Make it plain*) will stop killing civil rights workers and people who are simply engaged in the process of seeking their constitutional rights. (*Make it plain*)

The acceptable year of the Lord (*Yes*) is that year

when men will learn to live together as brothers. (*Yes, sir*)

The acceptable year of the Lord (*Yes*) is that year when men will keep their theology abreast with their technology.

The acceptable year of the Lord is that year when men will keep the ends for which they live abreast with the means by which they live. (*Yes*)

The acceptable year of the Lord is that year (*That year*) when men will keep their morality abreast with their mentality.

The acceptable year of the Lord is that year (*Yes*) when all of the leaders of the world will sit down at the conference table (*Make it plain*) and realize that unless mankind puts an end to war, war will put an end to mankind. (*Yes*)

The acceptable year of the Lord [*Clap*] is that year when men will beat their swords into plowshares, (*Yes*) and their spears into pruning hooks; and nations will not rise up against nations, neither will they study war anymore. (*Yes*)

The acceptable year of the Lord is that year (*That year*) when men will allow justice to roll down like waters, and righteousness like a mighty stream. (*Yes*)

The acceptable year of the Lord is that year when we will send to Congress and to state houses of our nation (*Yes, sir*) men who will do justly, (*Yes*) who will love mercy, (*Yes*) and who will walk humbly with their God. (*Yes*)

The acceptable year of the Lord is that year (*Yes, sir*)

when every valley shall be exalted, and every mountain will be made low; the rough places would be made plain, and the crooked places straight; and the glory of the Lord shall be revealed, and all flesh shall see it together.

The acceptable year of the Lord is that year when men will do unto others as they will have others do unto themselves. (*Yes*)

The acceptable year of the Lord is that year when men will love their enemies, (*Yes*) bless them that curse them, pray for them that despitefully use them.

The acceptable year of the Lord is that year when men discover that out of one blood God made all men to dwell upon the face of the earth. (*Yes*)

The acceptable year of the Lord is that year when every knee shall bow and every tongue shall confess the name of Jesus. And everywhere men will cry out, "Hallelujah, hallelujah! The kingdom of this world has become the kingdom of our Lord and his Christ, and he shall reign forever and ever. Hallelujah, hallelujah!"

The acceptable year of the Lord is God's year. (*Yes*)

These are our guidelines, and if we will only follow the guidelines, we will be ready for God's kingdom, (*Yes*) we will be doing what God's church is called to do. We won't be a little social club. (*Make it plain*) We won't be a little entertainment center. But we'll be about the serious business (*Yes*) of bringing God's kingdom to this earth.

It seems that I can hear the God of the universe smiling and speaking to this church, saying, "You are a great church (*Glory to God*) because I was hungry and ye fed me. You are a great church because I was naked and ye clothed me. You are a great church because I was sick and ye visited me. You are a great church because I was in prison and ye gave me consolation by visiting me." (*Yes, sir*) And this is the church that's going to save this world. "The spirit of the Lord is upon me (*Yes*) because he has anointed me to heal the brokenhearted, to set at liberty them that are captive, (*Amen*) and to preach the acceptable year of the Lord."

DELIVERED AT EBENEZER BAPTIST CHURCH, ATLANTA, GEORGIA, 5 JUNE 1966 [MLKEC]

# THE THREE
# DIMENSIONS OF A
# COMPLETE LIFE

INTRODUCTION BY FATHER THEODORE HESBURGH

ne of the great deceptions that one must guard against in reading the sermons of Martin Luther King is that on the surface they appear so simple as to be simplistic. This particular sermon starts out talking about a complete life being made up of length, breadth, and height. How simplistic can one be? However, if you read carefully and listen intently, the message is very deep, very essential, and even at times mystical.

There are moments when Martin speaks very simply in the black jargon of the day, mixing up grammar, tenses, and proper grammatical connections. Then, once he has the attention of the listener, who is hearing familiar words, he lifts them into the sky, to heights of idealism, to the very core of the Christian life, and buttons it all down by constantly quoting Jesus, who spoke the same way and made the great mysteries of the universe seem fairly simple and certainly understandable.

Martin was never pedantic, yet he was always teaching. The spirit of the gospel runs deeply through each line of this sermon, and the familiar citations from the Lord make the words sound very much like family talk. In the midst of simple conversation about life and the things of God, he suddenly pulls in (without identifying its author) a very profound statement from Saint Augustine about the restlessness in our hearts. No need to show off his wide-ranging reading in theology. It is wonderful how scriptural wisdom and the actual biblical expressions of that wisdom flow simply in and out of the discussion, without adding a pedantic tone.

Martin was preaching in a time of enormous social concerns, social unrest, and deep-seated injustice that made it difficult for a black person to keep his or her self-respect. Martin simply says that life is about knowing and loving and respecting yourself—but not *just* that. That, he says, would be a selfish kind of life. One must not only be concerned about one's own inner peace but also what one might do for the good of others. This guidance is tied to the problems of those days: getting behind the social revolution, taking part in the civil rights movement, maintaining one's self-respect, and especially conquering fear of the present or even the future.

Dr. King reaches out directly to God and all that God has promised us and all that he gives us and all that we might expect if we give ourselves completely to him and leave ourselves in his hands. I imagine inner peace settling upon his congregation when Martin says that while he does not know how long he might live, he would do what he could for as long as he did.

These are very deep and pointed reflections on the times in which he lived and the difficulty of living in such times. In the end, he brings us back to God and to our faith in him, and he absolutely lyrically describes God and the universe he has made, which he cares so much about.

This is a real wedding of simplicity and eloquence, basic theological beliefs and deep theological purposes. Martin's range is from the earth to the heavens, and throughout the whole universe; yet he brings it all back in a simple way to the difficult life that all Christians must live in our troubled world.

---

FATHER THEODORE HESBURGH is the president of the University of Notre Dame and is a national figure because of his work with the federal government, ecumenism, and philanthropy.

# THE THREE DIMENSIONS OF A COMPLETE LIFE

─◆═◉═◆─

I want to use as the subject from which to preach: "The Three Dimensions of a Complete Life." (*All right*) You know, they used to tell us in Hollywood that in order for a movie to be complete, it had to be three-dimensional. Well, this morning I want to seek to get over to each of us that if life itself is to be complete, (*Yes*) it must be three-dimensional.

Many, many centuries ago, there was a man by the name of John who found himself in prison out on a lonely, obscure island called Patmos. (*Right, right*) And I've been in prison just enough to know that it's a lonely experience. (*That's right*) And when you are incarcerated in such a situation, you are deprived of almost every freedom, but the freedom to think, the freedom to pray, the freedom to reflect and to meditate. And while John was out on this lonely island in prison, (*That's right*) he lifted his vision to high heaven (*All right, he did*) and he saw, descending out of heaven, a new heaven (*All right*) and a new earth.

(*That's right*) Over in the twenty-first chapter of the Book of Revelation, it opens by saying, "And I saw a new heaven and a new earth. (*All right*) And I John saw the holy city, the new Jerusalem, (*All right*) coming down from God out of heaven." (*Oh yeah*)

And one of the greatest glories of this new city of God that John saw was its completeness. (*That's right*) It was not up on one side and down on the other, (*All right*) but it was complete in all three of its dimensions. (*Yes*) And so in this same chapter as we looked down to the sixteenth verse, John says, "The length and the breadth (*He did, he did*) and the height of it are equal." (*Yes, sir*) In other words, this new city of God, this new city of ideal humanity, is not an unbalanced entity (*No*) but is complete on all sides. (*Yes*) Now, I think John is saying something here in all of the symbolism of this text and the symbolism of this chapter. He's saying at bottom that life as it should be and life at its best (*Yeah*) is a life that is complete on all sides. (*That's right*)

And there are three dimensions of any complete life to which we can fitly give the words of this text: length, breadth, and height. (*Yes*) Now, the length of life as we shall use it here is the inward concern for one's own welfare. (*Yes*) In other words, it is that inward concern that causes one to push forward, to achieve his own goals and ambitions. (*All right*) The breadth of life as we shall use it here is the outward concern for the welfare of others. (*All right*) And the height of life is the upward reach for God. (*All right*)

Now, you got to have all three of these to have a complete life.

Now, let's turn for the moment to the length of life. I said that this is the dimension of life where we are concerned with developing our inner powers. (*Yeah*) In a sense this is the selfish dimension of life. There is such a thing as rational and healthy self-interest. (*Yeah*) A great Jewish rabbi, the late Joshua Leibman, wrote a book some years ago entitled *Peace of Mind*. And he has a chapter in that book entitled "Love Thyself Properly." And what he says in that chapter, in substance, is that before you can love other selves adequately, you've got to love your own self properly. (*All right*) You know, a lot of people don't love themselves. (*That's right*) And they go through life with deep and haunting emotional conflicts. So the length of life means that you must love yourself.

And you know what loving yourself also means? It means that you've got to accept yourself. (*All right*) So many people are busy trying to be somebody else. (*That's right*) God gave all of us something significant. And we must pray every day, asking God to help us to accept ourselves. (*Yeah*) That means everything. (*Yeah*) Too many Negroes are ashamed of themselves, ashamed of being black. (*Yes, sir*) A Negro got to rise up and say from the bottom of his soul, "I am somebody. (*Yes*) I have a rich, noble, and proud heritage. However exploited and however painful my history has been, I'm black, but I'm black and beautiful." (*Yeah*) This is what we've got to say. We've got to accept ourselves. (*Yeah*) And we must pray, "Lord, help me to accept myself every day; help me to accept my tools." (*Yeah*)

I remember when I was in college, I majored in sociology, and all sociology majors had to take a course that was required called statistics. And statistics can be very complicated. You've got to have a mathematical mind, a real knowledge of geometry, and you've got to know how to find the mean, the mode, and the median. I never will forget. I took this course and I had a fellow classmate who could just work that stuff out, you know. And he could do his homework in about an hour. We would often go to the lab or the workshop, and he would just work it out in about an hour, and it was over for him. And I was trying to do what he was doing; I was trying to do mine in an hour. And the more I tried to do it in an hour, the more I was flunking out in the course. And I had to come to a very hard conclusion. I had to sit down and say, "Now, Martin Luther King, Leif Cane has a better mind than you." (*That's right*) Sometimes you have to acknowledge that. (*That's right*) And I had to say to myself, "Now, he may be able to do it in an hour, but it takes me two or three hours to do it." I was not willing to accept myself. I was not willing to accept my tools and my limitations. (*Yeah*)

But you know, in life we're called upon to do this. A Ford car trying to be a Cadillac is absurd, but if a Ford will accept itself as a Ford, (*All right*) it can do many things that a Cadillac could never do: It can get in parking spaces that a Cadillac can never get in. [*Laughter*] And in life some of us are Fords and some of us are Cadillacs. (*Yes*) Moses says in "Green Pastures," "Lord, I ain't much, but I is all I got." [*Laughter*] The principle of self-acceptance is a basic principle in life.

Now, the other thing about the length of life: After accepting ourselves and our tools, we must discover what we are called to do. (*Oh yeah*) And once we discover it we should set out to do it with all of the strength and all of the power that we have in our systems. (*Yeah*) And after we've discovered what God called us to do, after we've discovered our life's work, we should set out to do that work so well that the living, the dead, or the unborn couldn't do it any better. (*Oh yeah*) Now, this does not mean that everybody will do the so-called big, recognized things of life. Very few people will rise to the heights of genius in the arts and the sciences, very few collectively will rise to certain professions. Most of us will have to be content to work in the fields and in the factories and on the streets. But we must see the dignity of all labor. (*That's right*)

When I was in Montgomery, Alabama, I went to a shoe shop quite often, known as the Gordon Shoe Shop. And there was a fellow in there that used to shine my shoes, and it was just an experience to witness this fellow shining my shoes. He would get that rag, you know, and he could bring music out of it. And I said to myself, "This fellow has a Ph.D. in shoe shining." (*That's right*)

What I'm saying to you this morning, my friends,

even if it falls your lot to be a street sweeper, go on out and sweep streets like Michelangelo painted pictures; sweep streets like Handel and Beethoven composed music; sweep streets like Shakespeare wrote poetry; (*Go ahead*) sweep streets so well that all the hosts of heaven and earth will have to pause and say, "Here lived a great street sweeper who swept his job well."

> If you can't be a pine on the top of a hill
> Be a scrub in the valley—but be
> The best little scrub on the side of the hill,
> Be a bush if you can't be a tree.

> If you can't be a highway just be a trail
> If you can't be the sun be a star;
> It isn't by size that you win or fail—
> Be the best of whatever you are.

And when you do this, when you do this, you've mastered the length of life. (*Yes*)

This onward push to the end of self-fulfillment is the end of a person's life. Now, don't stop here, though. You know, a lot of people get no further in life than the length. They develop their inner powers; they do their jobs well. But do you know, they try to live as if nobody else lives in the world but themselves? (*Yes*) And they use everybody as mere tools to get where they're going. (*Yes*) They don't love anybody but themselves. And the only kind of love that they really have for other people is utilitarian love. You know, they just love people that they can use. (*Well*)

A lot of people never get beyond the first dimension of life. They use other people as mere steps by which they can climb to their goals and their ambitions. These people don't work out well in life. They may go for a while, they may think they're making it all right, but there is a law. (*Oh yeah*) They call it the law of gravitation in the physical universe, and it works, it's final, it's inexorable: Whatever goes up can come down. You shall reap what you sow. (*Yeah*) God has structured the universe that way. (*Yeah*) And he who gets through life not concerned about others will be a subject, victim of this law.

So I move on and say that it is necessary to add breadth to length. Now, the breadth of life is the outward concern for the welfare of others, as I said. (*Yeah*) And a man has not begun to live until he can rise above the narrow confines of his own individual concerns to the broader concerns of all humanity. (*All right*)

One day Jesus told a parable. You will remember that parable. He had a man that came to him to talk with him about some very profound concerns. And they finally got around to the question, "Who is my neighbor?" (*All right*) And this man wanted to debate with Jesus. This question could have very easily ended up in thin air as a theological or philosophical debate. But you remember, Jesus immediately pulled that question out of thin air and placed it on a dangerous curve between Jerusalem and Jericho. (*He did, he did*)

He talked about a certain man who fell among thieves. (*Right*) Two men came by and they just kept going. And then finally another man came, a member of another race, who stopped and helped him. (*Oh yeah*) And that parable ends up saying that this good Samaritan was a great man; he was a good man because he was concerned about more than himself. (*Oh yeah*)

Now you know, there are many ideas about why the priest and the Levite passed and didn't stop to help that man. A lot of ideas about it. Some say that they were going to a church service, and they were running a little late, you know, and couldn't be late for church, so they kept going because they had to get down to the synagogue. And then there are others who would say that they were involved in the priesthood and consequently there was a priestly law which said that if you were going to administer the sacrament or what have you, you couldn't touch a human body twenty-four hours before worship. Now, there's another possibility. It is possible that they were going down to Jericho to organize a Jericho Road Improvement Association. That's another possibility. And they may have passed by because they felt that it was better to deal with the problem from the causal source rather than one individual victim. That's a possibility.

But you know, when I think about this parable, I think of another possibility as I use my imagination. It's possible that these men passed by on the other side because they were afraid. You know, the Jericho Road is a dangerous road. (*That's right*) I've been on it and I know. And I never will forget, Mrs. King and I were in the Holy Land some time ago. We rented a car and we drove from Jerusalem down to Jericho, a distance of about sixteen miles. You get on that Jericho road—I'm telling you it's a winding, curving, meandering road, very conducive for robbery. And I said to my wife, "Now I can see why Jesus used this road as the occasion for his parable." (*Yes*) Here you are when you start out in Jerusalem: You are twenty-two hundred feet above sea level, and when you get down to Jericho sixteen miles later—I mean, you have sixteen miles from Jerusalem—you're twelve hundred feet below sea level. During the days of Jesus that road came to the point of being known as the "Bloody Path." So when I think about the priest and the Levite, I think those brothers were afraid. (*All right*)

They were just like me. I was going out to my father's house in Atlanta the other day. He lives about three or four miles from me, and you go out there by going down Simpson Road. And then when I came back later that night—and brother, I can tell you, Simpson Road is a winding road. And a fellow was standing out there trying to flag me down. And I felt that he needed some help; I knew he needed help. [*Laughter*] But I didn't know it. I'll be honest with you, I kept going. [*Laughter*] I wasn't really willing to take the risk. (*That's right*)

I say to you this morning that the first question that the priest asked was the first question that I asked on that Jericho Road of Atlanta known as Simpson Road.

The first question that the Levite asked was "If I stop to help this man, what will happen to me?" (*That's right*) But the good Samaritan came by and he reversed the question. Not "What will happen to me if I stop to help this man?" but "What will happen to this man if I do not stop to help him?" This was why that man was good and great. He was great because he was willing to take a risk for humanity; he was willing to ask "What will happen to this man?" not "What will happen to me?" (*All right*)

This is what God needs today: (*Yes*) men and women who will ask "What will happen to humanity if I don't help? (*Oh yeah*) What will happen to the civil rights movement if I don't participate? (*Yes*) What will happen to my city if I don't vote? (*Oh yeah*) What will happen to the sick if I don't visit them?" This is how God judges people in the final analysis. (*Oh yeah*)

Oh, there will be a day, the question won't be "How many awards did you get in life?" Not that day. (*Yeah*) It won't be "How popular were you in your social setting?" That won't be the question that day. (*Yeah*) It will not ask how many degrees you've been able to get. (*All right*) The question that day will not be concerned with whether you are a "Ph.D." or a "no D." (*That's right*) It will not be concerned with whether you went to Morehouse or whether you went to "No House." (*Yes*) The question that day will not be "How beautiful is your house?" (*That's right*) The question that day will not be "How much money did you accumulate? How much did you have in stocks and bonds?" The question that day will not be "What kind of automobile did you have?" On that day the question will be "What did you do for others?" (*That's right*)

Now, I can hear somebody saying, "Lord, I did a lot of things in life. I did my job well; the world honored me for doing my job. (*Oh yeah*) I did a lot of things, Lord; I went to school and studied hard. I accumulated a lot of money, Lord; that's what I did." It seems as if I can hear the Lord of Life saying, "But I was hungry, and ye fed me not. (*That's right*) I was sick, and ye visited me not. I was naked, and ye clothed me not. I was in prison, and you weren't concerned about me. So get out of my face. What did you do for others?" (*That's right*) This is the breadth of life. (*Oh yeah*)

Somewhere along the way, we must learn that there is nothing greater than to do something for others. And this is the way I've decided to go the rest of my days. That's what I'm concerned about. John, if you and Bernard happen to be around when I come to the latter days and that moment to cross the Jordan, I want you to tell them that I made a request: I don't want a long funeral. In fact, I don't even need a eulogy (*No*) more than one or two minutes. (*All right*) I hope that I will live so well the rest of the days—I don't know how long I'll live, and I'm not concerned about that— but I hope I can live so well that the preacher can get up and say "He was faithful." (*Yes*) That's all, that's enough. (*That's right*) That's the sermon I'd like to hear: "Well done, my good and faithful servant. You've been faithful; you've been concerned about others."

(*That's right*) That's where I want to go from this point on the rest of my days. (*Oh yeah*) "He who is greatest among you shall be your servant." I want to be a servant. (*Yes*) I want to be a witness for my Lord, to do something for others.

And don't forget in doing something for others that you have what you have because of others. (*Yes, sir*) Don't forget that. We are tied together in life and in the world. (*Preach, preach*) And you may think you got all you got by yourself. (*Not all of it*) But you know, before you got out here to church this morning, you were dependent on more than half of the world. (*That's right*) You get up in the morning and go to the bathroom, and you reach over for a bar of soap, and that's handed to you by a Frenchman. You reach over for a sponge, and that's given to you by a Turk. You reach over for a towel, and that comes to your hand from the hands of a Pacific Islander. And then you go on to the kitchen to get your breakfast. You reach on over to get a little coffee, and that's poured in your cup by a South American. (*That's right*) Or maybe you decide that you want a little tea this morning, only to discover that that's poured in your cup by a Chinese. (*Yes*) Or maybe you want a little cocoa; that's poured in your cup by a West African. (*Yes*) Then you want a little bread and you reach over to get it, and that's given to you by the hands of an English-speaking farmer, not to mention the baker. (*That's right*) Before you get through eating breakfast in the morning, you're dependent on more than half the world. (*That's right*) That's the way God structured it; that's the way God structured this world. So let us be concerned about others because we are dependent on others. (*Oh yeah*)

But don't stop here either. (*No, sir*) You know, a lot of people master the length of life, and they master the breadth of life, but they stop right there. Now, if life is to be complete, we must move beyond our self-interest. We must move beyond humanity and reach up, way up for the God of the universe, whose purpose changeth not. (*Right*)

Now, a lot of people have neglected this third dimension. And you know, the interesting thing is a lot of people neglect it and don't even know they are neglecting it. They just get involved in other things. And you know, there are two kinds of atheism. Atheism is the theory that there is no God. Now, one kind is a theoretical kind, where somebody just sits down and starts thinking about it, and they come to a conclusion that there is no God. The other kind is a practical atheism, and that kind goes out of living as if there is no God. And you know there are a lot of people who affirm the existence of God with their lips, and they deny his existence with their lives. (*That's right*) You've seen these people who have a high blood pressure of creeds and an anemia of deeds. They deny the existence of God with their lives and they just become so involved in other things. They become so involved in getting a big bank account. (*Yeah*) They become so involved in getting a beautiful house, which we all should have. They become so involved in getting a beautiful car that they unconsciously just forget about God. (*Oh yeah*) There are those who become so involved in looking at the manmade lights of the city that they unconsciously forget to rise up and look at that great cosmic light and think about it—that gets up in the eastern horizon every morning and moves across the sky with a kind of symphony of motion and paints its technicolor across the blue—a light that man can never make. (*All right*) They become so involved in looking at the skyscraping buildings of the Loop of Chicago or Empire State Building of New York that they unconsciously forget to think about the gigantic mountains that kiss the skies as if to bathe their peaks in the lofty blue—something that man could never make. They become so busy thinking about radar and their television that they unconsciously forget to think about the stars that bedeck the heavens like swinging lanterns of eternity, those stars that appear to be shiny, silvery pins sticking in the magnificent blue pincushion. They become so involved in thinking about man's progress that they forget to think about the need for God's power in history. They end up going days and days not knowing that God is not with them. (*Go ahead*)

And I'm here to tell you today that we need God. (*Yes*) Modern man may know a great deal, but his knowledge does not eliminate God. (*Right*) And I tell you this morning that God is here to stay. A few theologians are trying to say that God is dead. And I've been asking them about it because it disturbs me to know that God died and I didn't have a chance to attend the funeral. They haven't been able to tell me yet the date of his death. They haven't been able to tell me yet who the coroner was that pronounced him dead. (*Preach, preach*) They haven't been able to tell me yet where he's buried.

You see, when I think about God, I know his name. He said somewhere, back in the Old Testament, "I want you to go out, Moses, and tell them 'I Am' sent you." (*That's right*) He said, just to make it clear, let them know that "my last name is the same as my first, 'I Am that I Am.' Make that clear. 'I Am.'" And God is the only being in the universe that can say "I Am" and put a period behind it. Each of us sitting here has to say "I am because of my parents; I am because of certain environmental conditions; I am because of certain hereditary circumstances; I am because of God." But God is the only being that can just say "I Am" and stop right there. "I Am that I Am." And he's here to stay. Let nobody make us feel that we don't need God. (*That's right*)

As I come to my conclusion this morning, I want to say that we should search for him. We were made for God, and we will be restless until we find rest in him. (*Oh yeah*) And I say to you this morning that this is the personal faith that has kept me going. (*Yes*) I'm not worried about the future. You know, even on this race question, I'm not worried. I was down in Alabama the other day, and I started thinking about the state of Alabama where we worked so hard and may continue to elect the Wallaces. And down in my home state of Georgia, we have another sick governor by the name of Lester Maddox. (*Yes*) And all of these things can get you confused, but they don't worry me. (*All right*) Because the God that I worship is a God that has a way of saying even to kings and even to governors, "Be still, and know that I am God." And God has not yet turned over this universe to Lester Maddox and Lurleen Wallace. Somewhere I read, "The earth is the Lord's and the fulness thereof," and I'm going on because I have faith in him. (*Oh yeah*) I do not know what the future holds, but I do know who holds the future. (*Yes*) And if he'll guide us and hold our hand, we'll go on in.

I remember down in Montgomery, Alabama, an experience that I'd like to share with you. When we were in the midst of the bus boycott, we had a marvelous old lady that we affectionately called Sister Pollard. She was a wonderful lady about seventy-two years old and she was still working at that age. (*Yes*) During the boycott she would walk every day to and from work. She was one that somebody stopped one day and said, "Wouldn't you like to ride?" And she said, "No." And then the driver moved on and stopped and thought, and backed up a little and said, "Well, aren't you tired?" She said, "Yes, my feets is tired, but my soul is rested." (*All right*)

She was a marvelous lady. And one week I can remember that I had gone through a very difficult week. (*Yes*) Threatening calls had come in all day and all night the night before, and I was beginning to falter and to get weak within and to lose my courage. (*All right*) And I never will forget that I went to the mass meeting that Monday night very discouraged and a little afraid, and wondering whether we were going to win the struggle. (*Oh yeah*) And I got up to make my talk that night, but it didn't come out with strength and power. Sister Pollard came up to me after the meeting and said, "Son, what's wrong with you?" Said, "You didn't talk strong enough tonight."

And I said, "Nothing is wrong, Sister Pollard, I'm all right."

She said, "You can't fool me." Said, "Something wrong with you." And then she went on to say these words: "Is the white folks doing something to you that you don't like?"

I said, "Everything is going to be all right, Sister Pollard."

And then she finally said, "Now, come close to me and let me tell you something one more time, and I want you to hear it this time." She said, "Now, I done told you we is with you." She said, "Now, even if we ain't with you, the Lord is with you." (*Yes*) And she concluded by saying, "The Lord's going to take care of you."

And I've seen many things since that day. I've gone through many experiences since that night in Montgomery, Alabama. Since that time Sister Pollard has died. Since that time I've been in more than eighteen jail cells. Since that time I've come perilously close to death at the hands of a demented Negro woman. Since that time I've seen my home bombed three times. Since that time I've had to live every day under the threat of death. Since that time I've had many frustrating and bewildering nights. But over and over again I can still hear Sister Pollard's words: "God's going to take care of you." So today I can face any man and any woman with my feet solidly placed on the ground and my head in the air because I know that when you are right, God will fight your battle.

"Darker yet may be the night, harder yet may be the fight. Just stand up for that which is right." It seems that I can hear a voice speaking even this morning, saying to all of us, "Stand up for what is right. Stand up for what is just. Lo, I will be with you even until the end of the world." Yes, I've seen the lightning flash. I've heard the thunder roll. I've felt sin-breakers dashing, trying to conquer my soul. But I heard the voice of Jesus saying still to fight on. He promised never to leave me, never to leave me alone. No, never alone. No, never alone. He promised never to leave me, never to leave me alone. And I go on in believing that. Reach out and find the breadth of life.

You may not be able to define God in philosophical terms. Men through the ages have tried to talk about him. (*Yes*) Plato said that he was the Architectonic Good. Aristotle called him the Unmoved Mover. Hegel called him the Absolute Whole. Then there was a man named Paul Tillich, who called him Being-Itself. We don't need to know all of these high-sounding terms. (*Yes*) Maybe we have to know him and discover him another way. (*Oh yeah*) One day you ought to rise up and say, "I know him because he's a lily of the valley." (*Yes*) He's a bright and morning star. (*Yes*) He's a rose of Sharon. He's a battle-ax in the time of Babylon. (*Yes*) And then somewhere you ought to just reach out and say, "He's my everything. He's my mother and my father. He's my sister and my brother. He's a friend to the friendless." This is the God of the universe. And if you believe in him and worship him, something will happen in your life. You will smile when others around you are crying. This is the power of God.

Go out this morning. Love yourself, and that means rational and healthy self-interest. You are commanded to do that. That's the length of life. Then follow that: Love your neighbor as you love yourself. You are commanded to do that. That's the breadth of life. And I'm going to take my seat now by letting you know that there's a first and even greater commandment: "Love the Lord thy God with all thy heart, (*Yeah*) with all thy soul, with all thy strength." I think the psychologist would just say "with all thy personality." And when you do that, you've got the breadth of life.

And when you get all three of these together, you can walk and never get weary. You can look up and see the morning stars singing together, and the sons of God shouting for joy. When you get all of these working together in your very life, judgment will roll down like waters, and righteousness like a mighty stream.

When you get all the three of these together, the lamb will lie down with the lion.

When you get all three of these together, you look up and every valley will be exalted, and every hill and mountain will be made low; the rough places will be made plain, and the crooked places straight; and the glory of the Lord shall be revealed and all flesh will see it together.

When you get all three of these working together, you will do unto others as you'd have them do unto you.

When you get all three of these together, you will recognize that out of one blood God made all men to dwell upon the face of the earth . . .*

+>=•=<+

DELIVERED AT NEW COVENANT BAPTIST CHURCH, CHICAGO, ILLINOIS, 9 APRIL 1967 [MLKEC]

---

*Recording interrupted.

# WHY JESUS CALLED A MAN A FOOL

INTRODUCTION BY REVEREND BILLY GRAHAM

r. King was my good friend. I had known his parents early in my ministry, when we held a Crusade in Atlanta. Since Dr. King's tragic death, his wife and family have continued as dear friends. Years ago, he came and spoke to our Team and his counsel was highly valued in our work for the Lord.

Dr. Martin Luther King, Jr., was known throughout the world as the most eloquent spokesperson of the civil rights movement, a champion of justice for all people and America's most effective nonviolent social leader of the twentieth century.

This gifted leader had a higher calling, which he describes with simple clarity: "I was a preacher of the gospel." Dr. King saw his greatest commitment and first calling in the ministry. His work as a civil rights leader was performed as part of his ministry for the Lord.

The sermon "Why Jesus Called a Man a Fool" reveals the insight and fervency of the preacher in an inspiring manner.

The vision, the dream, of Dr. King was for eternity while laboring in the present. The fool in the sermon failed to consider the ultimate end of life, which is to glorify God; nor did the fool acknowledge the source of all his blessings as being from the Lord God.

The application of the sermon is shown as a parallel to many of the problems that Dr. King encountered. It provides a fresh perspective on the civil rights struggle, along with lessons of courage, sharing, and the drive for justice.

Reading the sermon, we can sense the burden of the preacher and the heart he had for his people. The concept of the whole man reveals the concern of a true prophet.

A most vital point of this sermon is that a fool fails to depend upon the Lord. Dr. King's own "experience with God," related in the sermon, illustrates this.

It was not good enough to have knowledge about the God of his godly parents. In the heat of the civil rights movement, he relates, "I discovered then that religion had to become real to me and I had to know God for myself." And Dr. King came to know, as all of us can know, that "He promised never to leave me, never to leave me alone."

We honor Dr. Martin Luther King, Jr., by responding to the words of this preacher: avoiding the foolish and lifting our eyes, as he challenges us to do, to the vision of the coming of the glory of the Lord.

---

THE REVEREND BILLY GRAHAM is best known for his large-scale preaching tours, known as Crusades. The Reverend Graham first began preaching during World War II as an Evangelist with Youth for Christ. Crusade meetings in Los Angeles in 1949 launched Mr. Graham into international prominence as an Evangelist. He founded the Billy Graham Evangelistic Association in 1950.

# WHY JESUS
## CALLED A MAN
## A FOOL

As you know, we are involved in a difficult struggle. It was about a hundred and four years ago that Abraham Lincoln signed the Emancipation Proclamation, freeing the Negro from the bondage of physical slavery. And yet we stand here one hundred and four years later, and the Negro still isn't free. One hundred and four years later, we still have states like Mississippi and Alabama where Negroes are lynched at whim and murdered at will. One hundred and four years later, we must face the tragic fact that the vast majority of Negroes in our country find themselves perishing on a lonely island of poverty in the midst of a vast ocean of material prosperity. One hundred and four years later, fifty percent of the Negro families of our country are forced to live in substandard housing conditions, most of whom do not have wall-to-wall carpets; many of them are forced to live with wall-to-wall rats and roaches. One hundred and four years later, we find ourselves in a situation where even though we live in a nation founded on the prin-

ciple that all men are created equal, men are still arguing over whether the color of a man's skin determines
the content of his character. Now, this tells us that we
have a long, long way to go.

And I'm going to still need your prayer, I'm going to
still need your support. Because the period that we face
now is more difficult than any we've faced in the past.
But this morning I did not come to Mount Pisgah to
give a civil rights address; I have to do a lot of that; I
have to make numerous civil rights speeches. But before I was a civil rights leader, I was a preacher of the
gospel. This was my first calling and it still remains my
greatest commitment. You know, actually all that I do
in civil rights I do because I consider it a part of my
ministry. I have no other ambitions in life but to
achieve excellence in the Christian ministry. I don't
plan to run for any political office. I don't plan to do
anything but remain a preacher.

And what I'm doing in this struggle, along with
many others, grows out of my feeling that the preacher
must be concerned about the whole man. Not merely
his soul but his body. It's all right to talk about heaven.
I talk about it because I believe firmly in immortality.
But you've got to talk about the earth. It's all right to
talk about long white robes over yonder, but I want a
suit and some shoes to wear down here. It's all right to
talk about the streets flowing with milk and honey in
heaven, but I want some food to eat down here. It's
even all right to talk about the new Jerusalem. But one

day we must begin to talk about the new Chicago, the new Atlanta, the new New York, the new America.

And any religion that professes to be concerned about the souls of men (*Well*) and is not concerned about the slums that cripple the souls—the economic conditions that stagnate the soul (*Yes*) and the city governments that may damn the soul—is a dry, dead, do-nothing religion (*Yes. Amen*) in need of new blood. And so I come to you this morning to talk about some of the great insights from the scripture in general, and from the New Testament in particular. I want to use as a subject from which to preach: "Why Jesus Called a Man a Fool." (*Yeah*) "Why Jesus Called a Man a Fool." (*Yeah*)

I want to share with you a dramatic little story from the gospel as recorded by Saint Luke. It is a story of a man who by all standards (*Yes. Speak, Doc, speak*) of measurement would be considered a highly successful man. (*Yes*) And yet Jesus called him a fool. (*Yes*) If you will read that parable, you will discover that the central character in the drama is a certain rich man. (*Yes*) This man was so rich that his farm yielded tremendous crops. (*Yes*) In fact, the crops were so great that he didn't know what to do. It occurred to him that he had only one alternative, and that was to build some new and bigger barns so he could store all of his crops. (*Yes*) And then as he thought about this, he said, "Then I'm going to do something after I build my new and bigger barns." He said, "I'm going to store my goods and my fruit there, and then I'm going to say to my soul, 'Soul, thou hast much goods, laid up for many years.

Take thine ease, eat, drink, and be merry.'" (*Yes*) That brother thought that was the end of life. (*All right*)

But the parable doesn't end with that man making his statement. (*My Lord*) It ends by saying that God said to him, (*Yes*) "Thou fool. (*Yes*) Not next year, not next week, not tomorrow, but this night, (*Yes*) thy soul is required of thee." (*Yes*)

And so it was at the height of his prosperity he died. Look at that parable. (*Yes*) Think about it. (*Yes*) Think of this man: If he lived in Chicago today, he would be considered "a big shot." (*My Lord*) And he would abound with all of the social prestige and all of the community influence that could be afforded. (*Yes*) Most people would look up to him because he would have that something called money. (*Yes*) And yet a Galilean peasant had the audacity to call that man a fool. (*Yes*)

Now, Jesus didn't call the man a fool because he made his money in a dishonest fashion. There is nothing in that parable to indicate that this man was dishonest and that he made his money through conniving and exploitative methods. In fact, it seems to reveal that he had a modicum of humanity and that he was a very industrious man. He was a thrifty man, apparently a pretty hard worker. So Jesus didn't call him a fool because he got his money through dishonest means.

And there is nothing here to indicate that Jesus called this man a fool because he was rich. Jesus never made a universal indictment against all wealth. It's true that one day a rich young ruler came to him raising some questions about eternal life and Jesus said to him,

"Sell all." But in that case Jesus was prescribing individual surgery and not setting forth a universal diagnosis. You know, Jesus told another parable about a man who was very rich by the name of Dives, and Dives ended up going to hell. There was nothing indicating that Dives went to hell because he was rich. In fact, when Dives got in hell, he had a conversation with a man in heaven; and on the other end of that long-distance call between hell and heaven was Abraham in heaven. Now, if you go back to the Old Testament, you will discover that Abraham was a real rich man. It wasn't a millionaire in hell talking with a poor man in heaven; it was a little millionaire in hell talking with a multimillionaire in heaven. So that Jesus did not call this man a fool because he was rich.

I'd like for you to look at this parable with me and try to decipher the real reason that Jesus called this man a fool. Number one, Jesus called this man a fool because he allowed the means by which he lived to outdistance the ends for which he lived. (*Yes*) You see, each of us lives in two realms, the within and the without. (*Yeah*) Now, the within of our lives is that realm of spiritual ends expressed in art, literature, religion, and morality. The without of our lives is that complex of devices, of mechanisms and instrumentalities by means of which we live. The house we live in—that's part of the means by which we live. The car we drive, the clothes we wear, the money that we are able to accumulate—in short, the physical stuff that's necessary for us to exist. (*My Lord*)

Now, the problem is that we must always keep a line

of demarcation between the two. (*My Lord*) This man was a fool because he didn't do that. (*Yes*)

The other day in Atlanta, the wife of a man had an automobile accident. He received a call that the accident had taken place on the expressway. The first question he asked when he received the call: "How much damage did it do to my Cadillac?" He never asked how his wife was doing. Now, that man was a fool, because he had allowed an automobile to become more significant than a person. He wasn't a fool because he had a Cadillac, he was a fool because he worshiped his Cadillac. He allowed his automobile to become more important than God.

Somehow in life we must know that we must seek first the kingdom of God, and then all of those other things—clothes, houses, cars—will be added unto us. But the problem is, all too many people fail to put first things first. They don't keep a sharp line of demarcation between the things of life and the ends of life.

And so this man was a fool because he allowed the means by which he lived to outdistance the ends for which he lived. He was a fool because he maximized the minimum and minimized the maximum. This man was a fool because he allowed his technology to outdistance his theology. This man was a fool because he allowed his mentality to outrun his morality. Somehow he became so involved in the means by which he lived that he couldn't deal with the way to eternal matters. He didn't make contributions to civil rights. (*Yes*) He looked at suffering humanity and wasn't concerned about it. (*Yeah*)

He may have had great books in his library, but he

never read them. He may have had recordings of great music of the ages, but he never listened to [them]. He probably gave his wife mink coats, a convertible automobile, but he didn't give her what she needed most: love and affection. (*Yes*) He probably provided bread for his children, but he didn't give them any attention; he didn't really love them. Somehow he looked up at the beauty of the stars, but he wasn't moved by them. He had heard the glad tidings of philosophy and poetry, but he really didn't read it or comprehend it, or want to comprehend it. And so this man justly deserved his title. He was an eternal fool. (*Yes*) He allowed the means by which he lived to outdistance the ends for which he lived. (*Yes*)

Now, number two, this man was a fool because he failed to realize his dependence on others. (*Yes*) Now, if you read that parable in the book of Luke, you will discover that this man utters about sixty words. And do you know in sixty words he said "I" and "my" more than fifteen times? (*My Lord*) This man was a fool because he said "I" and "my" so much until he lost the capacity to say "we" and "our." (*Yes*) He failed to realize that he couldn't do anything by himself. This man talked like he could build the barns by himself, like he could till the soil by himself. And he failed to realize that wealth is always a result of the commonwealth.

Maybe you haven't ever thought about it, but you can't leave home in the morning without being dependent on most of the world. You get up in the morning, and you go to the bathroom and you reach over for a sponge, and that's even given to you by a Pacific Islander. You reach over for a towel, and that's given to you by a Turk. You reach down to pick up your soap, and that's given to you by a Frenchman. Then after dressing, you rush to the kitchen and you decide this morning that you want to drink a little coffee; that's poured in your cup by a South American. Or maybe this morning you prefer tea; that's poured in your cup by a Chinese. Or maybe you want cocoa this morning; that's poured in your cup by a West African. Then you reach over to get your toast, and that's given to you at the hands of an English-speaking farmer, not to mention the baker. Before you finish eating breakfast in the morning you are dependent on more than half of the world.

And oh my friends, I don't want you to forget it. No matter where you are today, somebody helped you to get there. (*Yes*) It may have been an ordinary person, doing an ordinary job in an extraordinary way. Some few are able to get some education; you didn't get it by yourself. Don't forget those who helped you come over.

There is a magnificent lady, with all of the beauty of blackness and black culture, by the name of Marian Anderson that you've heard about and read about and some of you have seen. She started out as a little girl singing in the choir of the Union Baptist Church in Philadelphia, Pennsylvania. And then came that glad day when she made it. And she stood in Carnegie Hall, with the Philharmonic Orchestra in the background in New York, singing with the beauty that is matchless. Then she came to the end of that concert, singing "Ave

Maria" as nobody else can sing it. And they called her back and back and back and back again, and she finally ended by singing "Nobody Knows de Trouble I Seen." And her mother was sitting out in the audience, and she started crying; tears were flowing down her cheeks. And the person next to her said, "Mrs. Anderson, why are you crying? Your daughter is scoring tonight. The critics tomorrow will be lavishing their praise on her. Why are you crying?"

And Mrs. Anderson looked over with tears still flowing and said, "I'm not crying because I'm sad, I'm crying for joy." She went on to say, "You may not remember; you wouldn't know. But I remember when Marian was growing up, and I was working in a kitchen till my hands were all but parched, my eyebrows all but scalded. I was working there to make it possible for my daughter to get an education. And I remember one day Marian came to me and said, 'Mother, I don't want to see you having to work like this.' And I looked down and said, 'Honey, I don't mind it. I'm doing it for you and I expect great things of you.' "

And finally one day somebody asked Marian Anderson in later years, "Miss Anderson, what has been the happiest moment of your life? Was it the moment that you had your debut in Carnegie Hall in New York?" She said, "No, that wasn't it." "Was it the moment you stood before the kings and queens of Europe?" "No, that wasn't it." "Well, Miss Anderson, was it the moment that Sibelius of Finland declared that his roof was too low for such a voice?" "No, that wasn't it." "Miss Anderson, was it the moment that Toscanini said that a voice like yours comes only once in a century?" "No, that wasn't it." "What was it then, Miss Anderson?" And she looked up and said quietly, "The happiest moment in my life was the moment that I could say, 'Mother, you can stop working now.'" Marian Anderson realized that she was where she was because somebody helped her to get there.

In a larger sense we've got to see this in our world today. Our white brothers must see this; they haven't seen it up to now. The great problem facing our nation today in the area of race is that it is the black man who to a large extent produced the wealth of this nation. (*All right*) And the nation doesn't have sense enough to share its wealth and its power with the very people who made it so. (*All right*) And I know what I'm talking about this morning. (*Yes, sir*) The black man made America wealthy. (*Yes, sir*)

We've been here—that's why I tell you right now, I'm not going anywhere. They can talk, these groups; some people talking about a separate state, or go back to Africa. I love Africa, it's our ancestral home. But I don't know about you. My grandfather and my great-grandfather did too much to build this nation for me to be talking about getting away from it. [*Applause*] Before the Pilgrim fathers landed at Plymouth in 1620, we were here. (*Oh yeah*) Before Jefferson etched across the pages of history the majestic words of the Declaration of Independence, we were here. (*All right*) Before the beautiful words of "The Star-Spangled Banner" were written, we were here. (*Yeah*) For more than two centuries, our forebears labored here without wages. They made cotton king. With their hands and with their backs and with their labor, they built the sturdy docks, the stout factories, the impressive mansions of the South. (*My Lord*)

Now this nation is telling us that we can't build. Negroes are excluded almost absolutely from the building trades. It's lily white. Why? Because these jobs pay six, seven, eight, nine, and ten dollars an hour, and they don't want Negroes to have it. [*Applause*] And I feel that if something doesn't happen soon, and something massive, the same indictment will come to America: "Thou fool!"

That man said he didn't know what to do with his goods, he had so many. Oh, I wish I could have advised him. (*My Lord*) A lot of places to go, and there were a lot of things that could be done. There were hungry stomachs that needed to be filled; there were empty pockets that needed access to money. America today, my friends, is also rich in goods. (*My Lord*) We have our barns, and every day our rich nation is building new and larger and greater barns. You know, we spend millions of dollars a day to store surplus food. But I want to say to America, "I know where you can store that food free of charge: (*Yes*) in the wrinkled stomachs of the millions of God's children in Asia and Africa and South America and in our own nation who go to bed hungry tonight." (*Yes*)

There are a lot of fools around. (*Lord help him*) Because they fail to realize their dependence on others.

Finally, this man was a fool because he failed to realize his dependence on God. (*Yeah*) Do you know that man talked like he regulated the seasons? That man talked like he gave the rain to grapple with the fertility of the soil. (*Yes*) That man talked like he provided the dew. He was a fool because he ended up acting like he was the Creator, (*Yes*) instead of a creature. (*Amen*)

And this man-centered foolishness is still alive today. In fact, it has gotten to the point today that some are even saying that God is dead. The thing that bothers me about it is that they didn't give me full information, because at least I would have wanted to attend God's funeral. And today I want to ask: Who was the coroner that pronounced him dead? I want to raise a question: How long had he been sick? I want to know whether he had a heart attack or died of chronic cancer. These questions haven't been answered for me, and I'm going on believing and knowing that God is alive. You see, as long as love is around, God is alive. As long as justice is around, God is alive. There are certain conceptions of God that needed to die, but not God. You see, God is the supreme noun of life; he's not an adjective. He is the supreme subject of life; he's not a verb. He's the supreme independent clause; he's not a dependent clause. Everything else is dependent on him, but he is dependent on nothing.

One day Moses had to grapple with it, and God sent him out and told him to tell the people that " 'I Am' sent you." And Moses wondered about it, and he said, "Well, what am I to tell the folk?" [God] said, "Just go on and

tell them that 'I Am' sent you. And then if you need a little more information, let them know that my first name
is the same as my last, 'I Am that I Am.'" And God is the
only being in the universe that can say that "I Am" and
stop there. Whenever I say "I am," I have to say "I am because of"—because of my parents, because of my environment, because of hereditary circumstances. And each
of you has to say you are because of something. But God
is life supreme. Now God, the power that holds the universe in the palm of his hand, is the only being that can
say "I Am," and put a period there and never look back.
And don't be foolish enough to forget him.

You know, a lot of people are forgetting God. They
haven't done it theoretically, as others have done
through their theories—postulated through the God-
is-dead theology—but a lot of people just get involved
in other things. (*Yes*) And so many people become so
involved in their big bank accounts and in their beautiful expensive automobiles that they unconsciously
forget God. So many people become so involved in
looking at the manmade lights of the city that they forget to think about that great cosmic light that gets up
early in the morning in the eastern horizon and moves
with a kind of symphony of motion like a masterly
queen strolling across a mansion and paints its technicolor across the blue as it moves—a light that man
could never make. Some people have become so involved in looking at the skyscraping buildings of the
cities that they've forgotten to think about the gigantic
mountains, kissing the skies, as if to bathe their peaks

in the lofty blue—something that man could never make. So many people have become so involved in televisions and radar that they've forgotten to think about the beautiful stars that bedeck the heavens like swinging lanterns of eternity, standing there like shining silvery pins sticking in the magnificent blue pincushion—something that man could never make. So many people have come to feel that on their own efforts they can bring in a new world, but they've forgotten to think about the fact that the earth is the Lord's and the fulness thereof. And so they end up going over and over again without God.

But I tell you this morning, my friends, there's no way to get rid of him. And all of our new knowledge will not diminish God's being one iota. Neither the microcosmic compass of the atom nor the vast interstellar ranges of interstellar space can make God irrelevant for living in a universe, where stellar distance must be measured in light-years, where stars are five hundred million million miles from the earth, where heavenly bodies travel at incredible speeds. Modern man still has to cry out with the Psalmist, "When I behold the heavens, the work of thy hands and all that thou hast created; what is man, that thou is mindful of him? and the son of man, that thou hast remembered him?"

God is still around. One day you're going to need him. (*My Lord*) The problems of life will begin to overwhelm you, disappointments will begin to beat upon the door of your life like a tidal wave. (*Yes*) And if you don't have a deep and patient faith, (*Well*) you aren't going to be able to make it. (*My Lord*) I know this from my own experience. (*Yes*) The first twenty-five years of my life were very comfortable years, very happy years; didn't have to worry about anything. I have a marvelous mother and father. They went out of the way to provide everything for their children, basic necessities. I went right on through school, I never had to drop out to work or anything. And you know, I was about to conclude that life had been wrapped up for me in a Christmas package.

Now of course, I was religious; I grew up in the church. I'm the son of a preacher, I'm the great-grandson of a preacher, and the great-great-grandson of a preacher. My father is a preacher, my grandfather was a preacher, my great-grandfather was a preacher, my only brother is a preacher, my daddy's brother is a preacher. So I didn't have much choice, I guess. [*Laughter*] But I had grown up in the church, and the church meant something very real to me, but it was a kind of inherited religion, and I had never felt (*My Lord*) an experience with God in the way that you must have it if you're going to walk the lonely paths of this life. (*Yeah*) Everything was done, and if I had a problem I could always call Daddy, my earthly father; things were solved.

But one day after finishing school, I was called to a little church down in Montgomery, Alabama, and I started preaching there. Things were going well in that church; it was a marvelous experience. But one day a year later, a lady by the name of Rosa Parks decided that she wasn't going to take it any longer. She stayed in a bus seat, and you may not remember it because (*I do*) it's way back now several years, but it was the beginning of a movement where fifty thousand black men and women refused absolutely to ride the city buses. And we walked together for 381 days. (*Yes, sir*) That's what we got to learn in the North: Negroes have to learn to stick together. We stuck together. [*Applause*] We sent out the call and no Negro rode the buses. It was one of the most amazing things I've ever seen in my life. And the people of Montgomery asked me to serve as the spokesman, and as the president of the new organization—the Montgomery Improvement Association that came into being to lead the boycott; I couldn't say no. And then we started our struggle together. (*Yeah*)

Things were going well for the first few days, but then about ten or fifteen days later, after the white people in Montgomery knew that we meant business, they started doing some nasty things. (*Yes*) They started making nasty telephone calls, and it came to the point that some days more than forty telephone calls would come in, threatening my life, the life of my family, the lives of my children. I took it for a while in a strong manner.

But I never will forget one night very late. It was around midnight. And you can have some strange experiences at midnight. (*Yes, sir*) I had been out meeting with the steering committee all that night. And I came home, and my wife was in the bed, and I immediately crawled into bed to get some rest to get up early the next morning to try to keep things going. And immediately the telephone started ringing and I picked it up.

On the other end was an ugly voice. That voice said to me, in substance, "Nigger, we are tired of you and your mess now. And if you aren't out of this town in three days, we're going to blow your brains out and blow up your house." (*Lord Jesus*)

I'd heard these things before, but for some reason that night it got to me. I turned over and I tried to go to sleep, but I couldn't sleep. (*Yes*) I was frustrated, bewildered. And then I got up and went back to the kitchen and I started warming some coffee, thinking that coffee would give me a little relief. And then I started thinking about many things. I pulled back on the theology and philosophy that I had just studied in the universities, trying to give philosophical and theological reasons for the existence and the reality of sin and evil, but the answer didn't quite come there. I sat there and thought about a beautiful little daughter who had just been born about a month earlier. We have four children now, but we only had one then. She was the darling of my life. I'd come in night after night and see that little gentle smile. And I sat at that table thinking about that little girl and thinking about the fact that she could be taken away from me any minute. (*Go ahead*) And I started thinking about a dedicated, devoted, and loyal wife who was over there asleep. (*Yes*) And she could be taken from me, or I could be taken from her. And I got to the point that I couldn't take it any longer; I was weak. (*Yes*)

Something said to me, You can't call on Daddy now; he's up in Atlanta a hundred and seventy-five miles away. (*Yes*) You can't even call on Mama now. (*My*

*Lord*) You've got to call on that something in that person that your daddy used to tell you about. (*Yes*) That power that can make a way out of no way. (*Yes*) And I discovered then that religion had to become real to me and I had to know God for myself. (*Yes, sir*) And I bowed down over that cup of coffee—I never will forget it. (*Yes, sir*) And oh yes, I prayed a prayer and I prayed out loud that night. (*Yes*) I said, "Lord, I'm down here trying to do what's right. (*Yes*) I think I'm right; I think the cause that we represent is right. (*Yes*) But Lord, I must confess that I'm weak now; I'm faltering; I'm losing my courage. (*Yes*) And I can't let the people see me like this because if they see me weak and losing my courage, they will begin to get weak." (*Yes*) I wanted tomorrow morning to be able to go before the executive board with a smile on my face.

And it seemed at that moment that I could hear an inner voice saying to me, (*Yes*) "Martin Luther, (*Yes*) stand up for righteousness, (*Yes*) stand up for justice, (*Yes*) stand up for truth. (*Yes*) And lo, I will be with you, (*Yes*) even until the end of the world."

And I'll tell you, I've seen the lightning flash. I've heard the thunder roll. I felt sin-breakers dashing, trying to conquer my soul. But I heard the voice of Jesus saying still to fight on. He promised never to leave me, never to leave me alone. No, never alone. No, never alone. He promised never to leave me, (*Never*) never to leave me alone.

And I'm going on in believing in him. (*Yes*) You'd better know him, and know his name, and know how to call his name. (*Yes*) You may not know philosophy. You may not be able to say with Alfred North Whitehead that he's the Principle of Concretion. You may not be able to say with Hegel and Spinoza that he is the Absolute Whole. You may not be able to say with Plato that he's the Architectonic Good. You may not be able to say with Aristotle that he's the Unmoved Mover.

But sometimes you can get poetic about it if you know him. You begin to know that our brothers and sisters in distant days were right. Because they did know him as a rock in a weary land, as a shelter in the time of starving, as my water when I'm thirsty, and then my bread in a starving land. And then if you can't even say that, sometimes you may have to say, "He's my everything. He's my sister and my brother. He's my mother and my father." If you believe it and know it, you never need walk in darkness.

Don't be a fool. Recognize your dependence on God. (*Yes, sir*) As the days become dark and the nights become dreary, realize that there is a God who rules above.

And so I'm not worried about tomorrow. I get weary every now and then. The future looks difficult and dim, but I'm not worried about it ultimately because I have faith in God. Centuries ago Jeremiah raised a question, "Is there no balm in Gilead? Is there no physician there?" He raised it because he saw the good people suffering so often and the evil people prospering. (*Yes, sir*) Centuries later our slave foreparents came along. (*Yes, sir*) And they too saw the injustices of life, and had nothing to look forward to morning after morning but the rawhide whip of the overseer, long rows of cotton in the sizzling heat. But they did an amazing thing. They looked back across the centuries and they took Jeremiah's question mark and straightened it into an exclamation point. And they could sing, "There is a balm in Gilead to make the wounded whole. (*Yes*) There is a balm in Gilead to heal the sin-sick soul." And there is another stanza that I like so well: "Sometimes (*Yeah*) I feel discouraged." (*Yes*)

And I don't mind telling you this morning that sometimes I feel discouraged. (*All right*) I felt discouraged in Chicago. As I move through Mississippi and Georgia and Alabama, I feel discouraged. (*Yes, sir*) Living every day under the threat of death, I feel discouraged sometimes. Living every day under extensive criticisms, even from Negroes, I feel discouraged sometimes. [*Applause*] Yes, sometimes I feel discouraged and feel my work's in vain. But then the Holy Spirit (*Yes*) revives my soul again. "There is a balm in Gilead to make the wounded whole. There is a balm in Gilead to heal the sin-sick soul." God bless you. [*Applause*]

DELIVERED AT MOUNT PISGAH MISSIONARY BAPTIST CHURCH, CHICAGO, ILLINOIS, 27 AUGUST 1967 [MLKEC]

# THE
# DRUM MAJOR
# INSTINCT

INTRODUCTION BY REVEREND ROBERT M. FRANKLIN

hat kind of man was he? He surren-
dered his life to God and became an
extraordinary representative of Christianity serving the common good.
Curiously, he offered instructions about his own funeral service. Do you recall what metaphor he used to
describe himself in that sermon? He characterized his
life and public ministry as that of a "drum major for
justice."

You can imagine my keen interest in the sermon ti-
tled "The Drum Major Instinct." I thought, perhaps,
this sermon would open a window into Dr. King's own
self-understanding. It certainly does that, but it goes
even further, offering profound insights into the great
contest each of us faces on a daily basis.

The great teachers of preaching and the dramatic
arts remind us that every good sermon, play, or story
has at least three elements: situation, complication,

and resolution. In this sermon, we encounter the theological wisdom, social scientific insight, and the literary artistry of Dr. King. He lays out the situation of a couple of familiar biblical characters who are driven by their hungry egos. Then he complicates the situation of the listener by suggesting that this hunger is common to humans as individuals and in larger social groups. We all have the drum major instinct, the desire to be in front, leading the parade. He uses this metaphor brilliantly to describe the negative manifestations of the instinct, such as racism, class oppression, and militarism. And he opens the window further by mentioning his own need for attention, offering a vulnerable, even humorous portrait of himself. The preacher invites us to witness and celebrate the resolution in the text. It is a resolution that we do not expect. Like Jesus, Dr. King knew how to tell a good story and how to surprise his listeners.

This sermon resonates loud and clear in a culture dominated by rugged individualists driven by the quest for greatness and immortality. We do not want to hear the words of this sermon because we insist upon being in front of the parade. But by describing himself as a drum major for justice, Dr. King surprises us by offering a formula for how our aspirations and ambitions can find legitimate and noble expression.

As president of America's largest black theological seminary, I am delighted to celebrate and urge younger ministers to emulate the quality of thinking evident here and in other sermons in this collection. Insight from psychology, sociology, economics, and theology are brought into a stimulating and practical mix. Dr. King was a religious intellectual, and, given the power of the action that accompanied the ideas, he may very well be the greatest religious intellectual of the twentieth century. Our culture is hungry for good preaching and for righteous public action. May we all be challenged by this invitation to become drum majors for justice and hope.

---

REVEREND ROBERT FRANKLIN is President of the Interdenominational Theological Center in Atlanta. His book *Another Day's Journey: Black Churches Confronting the American Crisis* was published in October 1997.

# THE
# DRUM MAJOR
# INSTINCT

This morning I would like to use as a subject from which to preach: "The Drum Major Instinct." And our text for [this] morning is taken from a very familiar passage in the tenth chapter as recorded by Saint Mark. Beginning with the thirty-fifth verse of that chapter, we read these words: "And James and John, the sons of Zebedee, came unto him saying, 'Master, we would that thou shouldest do for us whatsoever we shall desire.' And he said unto them, 'What would ye that I should do for you?' And they said unto him, 'Grant unto us that we may sit, one on thy right hand, and the other on thy left hand, in thy glory.' But Jesus said unto them, 'Ye know not what ye ask: Can ye drink of the cup that I drink of? And be baptized with the baptism that I am baptized with?' And they said unto him, 'We can.' And Jesus said unto them, 'Ye shall indeed drink of the cup that I drink of, and with the baptism that I am baptized withal shall ye be baptized: but to sit on my right hand and on my left hand is not mine to give; but it shall be given to them for whom it is prepared.'" And then Jesus goes on toward the end of that passage to say, "But so shall it not be among you: but whosoever will be great among you, shall be your servant: and whosoever of you will be the chiefest, shall be servant of all."

The setting is clear. James and John are making a specific request of the master. They had dreamed, as most of the Hebrews dreamed, of a coming king of Israel who would set Jerusalem free and establish his kingdom on Mount Zion, and in righteousness rule the world. And they thought of Jesus as this kind of king. And they were thinking of that day when Jesus would reign supreme as this new king of Israel. And they were saying, "Now, when you establish your kingdom, let one of us sit on the right hand and the other on the left hand of your throne."

Now, very quickly, we would automatically condemn James and John, and we would say they were selfish. Why would they make such a selfish request? But before we condemn them too quickly, let us look calmly and honestly at ourselves and we will discover that we too have those same basic desires for recognition, for importance. That same desire for attention, that same desire to be first. Of course, the other disciples got mad with James and John, and you could understand why, but we must understand that we have some of the same James and John qualities. And there is deep down within all of us an instinct. It's a kind of drum major instinct—a desire to be out front, a desire to lead the parade, a desire to be first. And it is something that runs the whole gamut of life.

And so before we condemn them, let us see that we all have the drum major instinct. We all want to be important, to surpass others, to achieve distinction, to lead the parade. Alfred Adler, the great psychoanalyst, contends that this is the dominant impulse. Sigmund Freud used to contend that sex was the dominant impulse, and Adler came with a new argument saying that this quest for recognition, this desire for attention, this desire for distinction is the basic impulse, the basic drive of human life, this drum major instinct.

And you know, we begin early to ask life to put us first. Our first cry as a baby was a bid for attention. And all through childhood the drum major impulse or instinct is a major obsession. Children ask life to grant them first place. They are a little bundle of ego. And they have innately the drum major impulse or the drum major instinct.

Now in adult life, we still have it, and we really never get by it. We like to do something good. And you know, we like to be praised for it. Now, if you don't believe that, you just go on living life, and you will discover very soon that you like to be praised. Everybody likes it, as a matter of fact. And somehow this warm glow we feel when we are praised or when our name is in print is something of the vitamin A to our ego. Nobody is unhappy when they are praised, even if they know they don't deserve it and even if they don't believe it. The only unhappy people about praise is when that praise is going too much toward somebody else. (*That's right*) But everybody likes to be praised because of this real drum major instinct.

Now, the presence of the drum major instinct is why so many people are "joiners." You know, there are some people who just join everything. And it's really a quest for attention and recognition and importance. And they get names that give them that impression. So you get your groups, and they become the "Grand Patron," and the little fellow who is henpecked at home needs a chance to be the "Most Worthy of the Most Worthy" of something. It is the drum major impulse and longing that runs the gamut of human life. And so we see it everywhere, this quest for recognition. And we join things, overjoin really, that we think that we will find that recognition in.

Now, the presence of this instinct explains why we are so often taken by advertisers. You know, those gentlemen of massive verbal persuasion. And they have a way of saying things to you that kind of gets you into buying. In order to be a man of distinction, you must drink this whiskey. In order to make your neighbors envious, you must drive this type of car. (*Make it plain*) In order to be lovely to love, you must wear this kind of lipstick or this kind of perfume. And you know, before you know it, you're just buying that stuff. (*Yes*) That's the way the advertisers do it.

I got a letter the other day, and it was a new magazine coming out. And it opened up, "Dear Dr. King: As you know, you are on many mailing lists. And you are categorized as highly intelligent, progressive, a lover of the arts and the sciences, and I know you will want to read what I have to say." Of course I did. After you said all of that and explained me so exactly, of course I wanted to read it. [*Laughter*]

But very seriously, it goes through life; the drum major instinct is real. (*Yes*) And you know what else it causes to happen? It often causes us to live above our means. (*Make it plain*) It's nothing but the drum major instinct. Do you ever see people buy cars that they can't even begin to buy in terms of their income? (*Amen*) [*Laughter*] You've seen people riding around in Cadillacs and Chryslers who don't earn enough to have a good Model-T Ford. (*Make it plain*) But it feeds a repressed ego.

You know, economists tell us that your automobile should not cost more than half of your annual income. So if you make an income of five thousand dollars, your car shouldn't cost more than about twenty-five hundred. That's just good economics. And if it's a family of two, and both members of the family make ten thousand dollars, they would have to make out with one car. That would be good economics, although it's often inconvenient. But so often, haven't you seen people making five thousand dollars a year and driving a car that costs six thousand? And they wonder why their ends never meet. [*Laughter*] That's a fact.

Now, the economists also say that your house shouldn't cost—if you're buying a house, it shouldn't cost more than twice your income. That's based on the economy and how you would make ends meet. So if you have an income of five thousand dollars, it's kind of difficult in this society. But say it's a family with an income of ten thousand dollars, the house shouldn't cost much more than twenty thousand. Well, I've seen folk making ten thousand dollars, living in a forty- and fifty-thousand-dollar house. And you know, they just barely make it. They get a check every month somewhere, and they owe all of that out before it comes in. Never have anything to put away for rainy days.

But now the problem is, it is the drum major instinct. And you know, you see people over and over again with the drum major instinct taking them over. And they just live their lives trying to outdo the Joneses. (*Amen*) They got to get this coat because this particular coat is a little better and a little better-looking than Mary's coat. And I got to drive this car because it's something about this car that makes my car a little better than my neighbor's car. (*Amen*) I know a man who used to live in a thirty-five-thousand-dollar house. And other people started building thirty-five-thousand-dollar houses, so he built a seventy-five-thousand-dollar house. And then somebody built a seventy-five-thousand-dollar house, and he built a hundred-thousand-dollar house. And I don't know where he's going to end up if he's going to live his life trying to keep up with the Joneses.

There comes a time that the drum major instinct can become destructive. (*Make it plain*) And that's where I want to move now. I want to move to the point of saying that if this instinct is not harnessed, it becomes a very dangerous, pernicious instinct. For instance, if it isn't harnessed, it causes one's personality to become distorted. I guess that's the most damaging aspect of it: what it does to the personality. If it isn't harnessed, you will end up day in and day out trying to deal with your ego problem by boasting. Have you ever heard people that—you know, and I'm sure you've met them—that really become sickening because they just sit up all the time talking about themselves. (*Amen*) And they just boast and boast and boast, and that's the person who has not harnessed the drum major instinct.

And then it does other things to the personality. It causes you to lie about who you know sometimes. (*Amen. Make it plain*) There are some people who are influence peddlers. And in their attempt to deal with the drum major instinct, they have to try to identify with the so-called big-name people. (*Yeah. Make it plain*) And if you're not careful, they will make you think they know somebody that they don't really know. (*Amen*) They know them well, they sip tea with them, and they this-and-that. That happens to people.

And the other thing is that it causes one to engage ultimately in activities that are merely used to get attention. Criminologists tell us that some people are driven to crime because of this drum major instinct. They don't feel that they are getting enough attention through the normal channels of social behavior, and so they turn to antisocial behavior in order to get attention, in order to feel important. (*Yeah*) And so they get that gun, and before they know it they robbed a bank in a quest for recognition, in a quest for importance.

And then the final great tragedy of the distorted personality is the fact that when one fails to harness this instinct, (*Glory to God*) he ends up trying to push others down in order to push himself up. (*Amen*) And whenever you do that, you engage in some of the most vicious activities. You will spread evil, vicious, lying gossip on people, because you are trying to pull them down in order to push yourself up. (*Make it plain*) And the great issue of life is to harness the drum major instinct.

Now, the other problem is, when you don't harness the drum major instinct—this uncontrolled aspect of it—is that it leads to snobbish exclusivism. It leads to snobbish exclusivism. (*Make it plain*) And you know, this is the danger of social clubs and fraternities—I'm in a fraternity; I'm in two or three—for sororities and all of these, I'm not talking against them. I'm saying it's the danger. The danger is that they can become forces of classism and exclusivism where somehow you get a degree of satisfaction because you are in something exclusive. And that's fulfilling something, you know—that I'm in this fraternity, and it's the best fraternity in the world, and everybody can't get in this fraternity. So it ends up, you know, a very exclusive kind of thing.

And you know, that can happen with the church; I know churches get in that bind sometimes. (*Amen. Make it plain*) I've been to churches, you know, and they say, "We have so many doctors, and so many schoolteachers, and so many lawyers, and so many businessmen in our church." And that's fine, because doctors need to go to church, and lawyers, and businessmen, teachers—they ought to be in church. But they say that—even the preacher sometimes will go all through that—they say that as if the other people don't count. (*Amen*)

And the church is the one place where a doctor ought to forget that he's a doctor. The church is the one place where a Ph.D. ought to forget that he's a Ph.D. (*Yes*) The church is the one place that the schoolteacher ought to forget the degree she has behind her name. The church is the one place where the lawyer ought to forget that he's a lawyer. And any church that violates the "whosoever will, let him come" doctrine is a dead, cold church, (*Yes*) and nothing but a little social club with a thin veneer of religiosity.

When the church is true to its nature, (*Whoo*) it says, "Whosoever will, let him come." (*Yes*) And it [is] not supposed to satisfy the perverted uses of the drum major instinct. It's the one place where everybody should be the same, standing before a common master and savior. (*Yes, sir*) And a recognition grows out of this—that all men are brothers because they are children (*Yes*) of a common father.

The drum major instinct can lead to exclusivism in one's thinking and can lead one to feel that because he has some training, he's a little better than that person who doesn't have it. Or because he has some economic security, that he's a little better than that person who doesn't have it. And that's the uncontrolled, perverted use of the drum major instinct.

Now the other thing is, that it leads to tragic—and we've seen it happen so often—tragic race prejudice. Many who have written about this problem—Lillian Smith used to say it beautifully in some of her books. And she would say it to the point of getting men and women to see the source of the problem. Do you know that a lot of the race problem grows out of the drum major instinct? A need that some people have to feel superior. A need that some people have to feel that they are first, and to feel that their white skin ordained them to be first. (*Make it plain today, 'cause I'm against it, so help me God*) And they have said over and over again in ways that we see with our own eyes. In fact, not too long ago, a man down in Mississippi said that God was a charter member of the White Citizens Council. And so God being the charter member means that everybody who's in that has a kind of divinity, a kind of superiority. And think of what has happened in history as a result of this perverted use of the drum major instinct. It has led to the most tragic prejudice, the most tragic expressions of man's inhumanity to man.

The other day I was saying, I always try to do a little converting when I'm in jail. And when we were in jail in Birmingham the other day, the white wardens and all enjoyed coming around the cell to talk about the race problem. And they were showing us where we were so wrong demonstrating. And they were showing us where segregation was so right. And they were showing us where intermarriage was so wrong. So I would get to preaching, and we would get to talking—calmly, because they wanted to talk about it. And then we got down one day to the point—that was the second or third day—to talk about where they lived, and how much they were earning. And when those brothers told me what they were earning, I said, "Now, you know what? You ought to be marching with us. [*Laughter*] You're just as poor as Negroes." And I said, "You are put in the position of supporting your oppressor, because through prejudice and blindness, you fail to see that the same forces that oppress Negores in American society oppress poor white people. (*Yes*) And all you are living on is the satisfaction of your skin being white, and the drum major instinct of thinking that you are somebody big because you are white. And you're so poor you can't send your children to school. You ought to be out here marching with every one of us every time we have a march."

Now, that's a fact. That the poor white has been put into this position, where through blindness and prejudice, (*Make it plain*) he is forced to support his oppressors. And the only thing he has going for him is the false feeling that he's superior because his skin is white—and can't hardly eat and make his ends meet week in and week out. (*Amen*)

And not only does this thing go into the racial struggle, it goes into the struggle between nations. And I would submit to you this morning that what is wrong in the world today is that the nations of the world are engaged in a bitter, colossal contest for supremacy. And if something doesn't happen to stop this trend, I'm sorely afraid that we won't be here to talk about Jesus Christ and about God and about brotherhood too many more years. (*Yeah*) If somebody doesn't bring an end to this suicidal thrust that we see in the world today, none of us are going to be around, because somebody's going to make the mistake through our senseless blunderings of dropping a nuclear bomb somewhere. And then another one is going to drop. And don't let anybody fool you, this can happen within a matter of seconds. (*Amen*) They have twenty-megaton bombs in Russia right now that can destroy a city as big as New York in three seconds, with everybody wiped away, and every building. And we can do the same thing to Russia and China.

But this is why we are drifting. And we are drifting there because nations are caught up with the drum major instinct. "I must be first." "I must be supreme." "Our nation must rule the world." (*Preach it*) And I am sad to say that the nation in which we live is the supreme culprit. And I'm going to continue to say it to America, because I love this country too much to see the drift that it has taken.

God didn't call America to do what she's doing in the world now. (*Preach it, preach it*) God didn't call America to engage in a senseless, unjust war as the war in Vietnam. And we are criminals in that war. We've committed more war crimes almost than any nation in the world, and I'm going to continue to say it. And we won't stop it because of our pride and our arrogance as a nation.

But God has a way of even putting nations in their place. (*Amen*) The God that I worship has a way of saying, "Don't play with me." (*Yes*) He has a way of saying, as the God of the Old Testament used to say to the Hebrews, "Don't play with me, Israel. Don't play with me, Babylon. (*Yes*) Be still and know that I'm God. And if you don't stop your reckless course, I'll rise up and break the backbone of your power." (*Yes*) And that can happen to America. (*Yes*) Every now and then I go back and read Gibbon's *Decline and Fall of the Roman Empire*. And when I come and look at America, I say to myself, The parallels are frightening. And we have perverted the drum major instinct.

But let me rush on to my conclusion, because I want you to see what Jesus was really saying. What was the answer that Jesus gave these men? It's very interesting. One would have thought that Jesus would have condemned them. One would have thought that Jesus would have said, "You are out of your place. You are selfish. Why would you raise such a question?"

But that isn't what Jesus did; he did something altogether different. He said in substance, "Oh, I see, you want to be first. You want to be great. You want to be important. You want to be significant. Well, you ought to be. If you're going to be my disciple, you must be." But he reordered priorities. And he said, "Yes, don't give up this instinct. It's a good instinct if you use it right. (*Yes*) It's a good instinct if you don't distort it and pervert it. Don't give it up. Keep feeling the need for being important. Keep feeling the need for being first. But I want you to be first in love. (*Amen*) I want you to be first in moral excellence. I want you to be first in generosity. That is what I want you to do."

And he transformed the situation by giving a new definition of greatness. And you know how he said it? He said, "Now brethren, I can't give you greatness. And really, I can't make you first." This is what Jesus said to James and John. "You must earn it. True greatness comes not by favoritism, but by fitness. And the right hand and the left are not mine to give, they belong to those who are prepared." (*Amen*)

And so Jesus gave us a new norm of greatness. If you want to be important—wonderful. If you want to be recognized—wonderful. If you want to be great—wonderful. But recognize that he who is greatest among you shall be your servant. (*Amen*) That's a new definition of greatness.

And this morning, the thing that I like about it: By giving that definition of greatness, it means that everybody can be great, (*Everybody*) because everybody can serve. (*Amen*) You don't have to have a college degree to serve. (*All right*) You don't have to make your subject and your verb agree to serve. You don't have to know about Plato and Aristotle to serve. You don't have to know Einstein's theory of relativity to serve. You don't have to know the second theory of thermodynamics in physics to serve. (*Amen*) You only need a heart full of grace, (*Yes, sir. Amen*) a soul generated by love. (*Yes*) And you can be that servant.

I know a man—and I just want to talk about him a minute, and maybe you will discover who I'm talking about as I go down the way (*Yeah*) because he was a great one. And he just went about serving. He was born in an obscure village, (*Yes, sir*) the child of a poor peasant woman. And then he grew up in still another obscure village, where he worked as a carpenter until he was thirty years old. (*Amen*) Then for three years, he just got on his feet, and he was an itinerant preacher. And he went about doing some things. He didn't have much. He never wrote a book. He never held an office. He never had a family. (*Yes*) He never owned a house. He never went to college. He never visited a big city. He never went two hundred miles from where he was born. He did none of the usual things that the world would associate with greatness. He had no credentials but himself.

He was only thirty-three when the tide of public opinion turned against him. They called him a rabble-rouser. They called him a troublemaker. They said he was an agitator. (*Glory to God*) He practiced civil disobedience; he broke injunctions. And so he was turned over to his enemies and went through the mockery of a trial. And the irony of it all is that his friends turned him over to them. (*Amen*) One of his closest friends denied him. Another of his friends turned him over to his enemies. And while he was dying, the people who killed him gambled for his clothing, the only possession that he had in the world. (*Lord help him*) When he was dead he was buried in a borrowed tomb, through the pity of a friend.

Nineteen centuries have come and gone and today he stands as the most influential figure that ever entered human history. All of the armies that ever marched, all the navies that ever sailed, all the parliaments that ever sat, and all the kings that ever reigned put together (*Yes*) have not affected the life of man on this earth (*Amen*) as much as that one solitary life. His name may be a familiar one. (*Jesus*) But today I can hear them talking about him. Every now and then somebody says, "He's King of Kings." (*Yes*) And again I can hear somebody saying, "He's Lord of Lords." Somewhere else I can hear somebody saying, "In Christ there is no East nor West." (*Yes*) And then they go on and talk about, "In him there's no North and South, but one great Fellowship of Love throughout the whole wide world." He didn't have anything. (*Amen*) He just went around serving and doing good.

This morning, you can be on his right hand and his left hand if you serve. (*Amen*) It's the only way in.

Every now and then I guess we all think realistically (*Yes, sir*) about that day when we will be victimized with what is life's final common denominator—that something that we call death. We all think about it. And every now and then I think about my own death and I think about my own funeral. And I don't think of it in a morbid sense. And every now and then I ask myself, "What is it that I would want said?" And I leave the word to you this morning.

If any of you are around when I have to meet my day, I don't want a long funeral. And if you get somebody to deliver the eulogy, tell them not to talk too long. (*Yes*) And every now and then I wonder what I want them to say. Tell them not to mention that I have a Nobel Peace Prize—that isn't important. Tell them not to mention that I have three or four hundred other awards—that's not important. Tell them not to mention where I went to school. (*Yes*)

I'd like somebody to mention that day that Martin Luther King, Jr., tried to give his life serving others. (*Yes*)

I'd like for somebody to say that day that Martin Luther King, Jr., tried to love somebody.

I want you to say that day that I tried to be right on the war question. (*Amen*)

I want you to be able to say that day that I did try to feed the hungry. (*Yes*)

And I want you to be able to say that day that I did try in my life to clothe those who were naked. (*Yes*)

I want you to say on that day that I did try in my life to visit those who were in prison. (*Lord*)

I want you to say that I tried to love and serve humanity. (*Yes*)

Yes, if you want to say that I was a drum major, say that I was a drum major for justice. (*Amen*) Say that I was a drum major for peace. (*Yes*) I was a drum major for righteousness. And all of the other shallow things will not matter. (*Yes*) I won't have any money to leave behind. I won't have the fine and luxurious things of life to leave behind. But I just want to leave a committed life behind. (*Amen*) And that's all I want to say.

If I can help somebody as I pass along,
If I can cheer somebody with a word or song,
If I can show somebody he's traveling wrong.
Then my living will not be in vain.

If I can do my duty as a Christian ought,
If I can bring salvation to a world once wrought,
If I can spread the message as the master taught,
Then my living will not be in vain.

Yes, Jesus, I want to be on your right or your left side, (*Yes*) not for any selfish reason. I want to be on your right or your left side, not in terms of some political kingdom or ambition. But I just want to be there in love and in justice and in truth and in commitment to others, so that we can make of this old world a new world.

DELIVERED AT EBENEZER BAPTIST CHURCH, ATLANTA, GEORGIA, 4 FEBRUARY 1968 [MLKEC]

# UNFULFILLED DREAMS

The time is important: Late in the winter of 1968, just a month before the assassin's relentless, long-traveling bullet finally found him. Approaching the darkness, living in the shadow, perhaps anticipating the elusive, eternal light, our brother needed to share these words of self-reflection, confession, and hope. Where better than at Ebenezer, with the congregation that had known him before he knew himself, the extended family of faith whose love could provide a space for their internationally renowned son to come home and say things that only a compassionate family could receive? He lectured and preached to others all over the world about magnificent dreams and even nightmares, but only at home did he find deep permission to share the soul-piercing reality of his most personal "unfulfilled dreams."

And yet, even (especially?) at home he found it difficult to share explicitly what was really in his heart. Was it just about being thirty-eight years old and realizing that he would probably never finish the work he had set out to do a decade earlier, the work of "redeeming the soul of America," the work of freeing black and white people, rich and poor people, to become their best, compassionate, courageous, democracy-loving selves? Was that what he wanted to say, to share with all the loving elders, all the young folks and family members in the choir? Was that what he wanted to say to Daddy behind him in the pulpit, to Momma at the organ?

Clearly, he needed to say something to this community of love about the schizophrenia in his soul, about the "civil war" going on in his heart, about his own life's troubling connection to the poet's words: "I see and approve the better things of life, but the evil things I do." He needed to confess how deeply he had failed himself and his own best possibilities, not only in the great public arena, where everyone could see his magnificent efforts at building temples of righteousness, justice, and peace. Where everyone could see the implacable opposition and the shadow of death that seemed to envelop him.

But here within the walls of Ebenezer's unpretentious beauty he needed to share the torment of his soul. Because an annealing flame of integrity burned within him far deeper than all the destructive fires of his inner civil war, he needed to speak out loud to the loving community. The closest he could come was this:

"You don't need to go out this morning saying that Martin Luther King is a saint. Oh, no . . . I want you to know this morning that I'm a sinner like all of God's children. But I want to be a good man."

There it was. Without necessarily knowing the details of his inner war, many of us had seen the evidence of that internal conflict in his face, heard it in his voice. We recognized it partly because it resembled so many of our own struggles. In that last year Martin looked more beleaguered, harassed, and desperate than I had ever seen him before, and it was clear that more than external enemies were at work. So at Ebenezer he needed to confess, because he really wanted to be "a good man"—indeed, he really was "a good man."

But the confession was not primarily to us, his friends, or to his congregation, as each of us struggled within the fires of our own fierce civil wars. Ultimately our brother was reaching out through us, beyond us, to his God, seeking to believe that in the ultimate divine encounter he would be received with love, not as a failure but as one whose heart was right, one who carried the intention of righteousness at the center of his being, whose lifelong commitment would provide the deepest context for his unfulfilled personal and public dreams. That great hope was probably in his heart when he heard on April 4, for the last time in his life, the favorite, familiar song, "Precious Lord, take my hand, lead me on, let me stand. I am weak, I am tired, I am worn. Through the storm, through the night, lead me on to the light . . ."

I am convinced that Martin's faith in the precious, embracing, amazing love of God was rewarded. For it was several years after his death that I saw my friend in a dream. And it was indeed amazing: All the tension, all the dividedness that had been in his face, in his eyes, during those last months of life were now gone. Instead there was a quietness, a heartful peace that I had not seen since my first meeting with him in 1958. And in the dream, as he looked at me, even though he did not speak a word, I somehow knew he was saying, "It's all right, Vincent. It is well with my soul." Somehow that message seemed large enough for me, for all of us, forever.

---

DR. VINCENT HARDING, former executive director of the King Center, has been a professor at the Iliff School of Theology in Denver for over fifteen years and is currently co-chairperson of the Gandhi-Hamer-King Center for the Study of Religion and Democratic Renewal at Iliff. He has authored several books, including *Martin Luther King: The Inconvenient Hero* and *There Is a River.*

# Unfulfilled
# Dreams

◆✦◆

I want to preach this morning from the subject: "Unfulfilled Dreams." "Unfulfilled Dreams." My text is taken from the eighth chapter of First Kings. Sometimes it's overlooked. It is not one of the most familiar passages in the Old Testament. But I never will forget when I first came across it. It struck me as a passage having cosmic significance because it says so much in so few words about things that we all experience in life. David, as you know, was a great king. And the one thing that was foremost in David's mind and in his heart was to build a great temple. The building of the temple was considered to be the most significant thing facing the Hebrew people, and the king was expected to bring this into being. David had the desire; he started.

And then we come to that passage over in the eighth chapter of First Kings, which reads, "And it was in the heart of David my father to build an house for the name of the Lord God of Israel. And the Lord said unto David my father, 'Whereas it was in thine heart to build an house unto my name, thou didst well that it was within thine heart.'" And that's really what I want to talk about this morning: It is well that it was within thine heart. As if to say, "David, you will not be able to finish the temple. You will not be able to build it. But I just want to bless you, because it was within thine heart. Your dream will not be fulfilled. The majestic hopes that guided your days will not be carried out in terms of an actual temple coming into being that you were able to build. But I bless you, David, because it was within thine heart. You had the desire to do it; you had the intention to do it; you tried to do it; you started to do it. And I bless you for having the desire and the intention in your heart. It is well that it was within thine heart."

So many of us in life start out building temples: temples of character, temples of justice, temples of peace. And so often we don't finish them. Because life is like Schubert's "Unfinished Symphony." At so many points we start, we try, we set out to build our various temples. And I guess one of the great agonies of life is that we are constantly trying to finish that which is unfinishable. We are commanded to do that. And so we, like David, find ourselves in so many instances having to face the fact that our dreams are not fulfilled.

Now, let us notice first that life is a continual story of shattered dreams. Mahatma Gandhi labored for years and years for the independence of his people. And through a powerful nonviolent revolution he was able to win that independence. For years the Indian people had been dominated politically, exploited economically, segregated and humiliated by foreign powers, and Gandhi struggled against it. He struggled to unite his own people, and nothing was greater in his mind than to have India's one great, united country moving toward a higher destiny. This was his dream.

But Gandhi had to face the fact that he was assassinated and died with a broken heart, because that nation that he wanted to unite ended up being divided between India and Pakistan as a result of the conflict between the Hindus and the Moslems. Life is a long, continual story of setting out to build a great temple and not being able to finish it.

Woodrow Wilson dreamed a dream of a League of Nations, but he died before the promise was delivered.

The Apostle Paul talked one day about wanting to go to Spain. It was Paul's greatest dream to go to Spain, to carry the gospel there. Paul never got to Spain. He ended up in a prison cell in Rome. This is the story of life.

So many of our forebears used to sing about freedom. And they dreamed of the day that they would be able to get out of the bosom of slavery, the long night of injustice. (*Yes, sir*) And they used to sing little songs: "Nobody knows de trouble I seen, nobody knows but Jesus." (*Yes*) They thought about a better day as they dreamed their dream. And they would say, "I'm so glad the trouble don't last always. (*Yeah*) By and by, by and by, I'm going to lay down my heavy load." (*Yes, sir*) And they used to sing it because of a powerful dream.

(*Yes*) But so many died without having the dream fulfilled.

And each of you this morning in some way is building some kind of temple. The struggle is always there. It gets discouraging sometimes. It gets very disenchanting sometimes. Some of us are trying to build a temple of peace. We speak out against war, we protest, but it seems that your head is going against a concrete wall. It seems to mean nothing. (*Glory to God*) And so often as you set out to build the temple of peace you are left lonesome; you are left discouraged; you are left bewildered.

Well, that is the story of life. And the thing that makes me happy is that I can hear a voice crying through the vista of time, saying: "It may not come today or it may not come tomorrow, but it is well that it is within thine heart. (*Yes*) It's well that you are trying." (*Yes it is*) You may not see it. The dream may not be fulfilled, but it's just good that you have a desire to bring it into reality. (*Yes*) It's well that it's in thine heart.

Thank God this morning that we do have hearts to put something meaningful in. Life is a continual story of shattered dreams.

Now, let me bring out another point. Whenever you set out to build a creative temple, whatever it may be, you must face the fact that there is a tension at the heart of the universe between good and evil. It's there: a tension at the heart of the universe between good and evil. (*Yes, sir*) Hinduism refers to this as a struggle between illusion and reality. Platonic philosophy used to refer to it as a tension between body and soul. Zoroastrianism, a religion of old, used to refer to it as a tension between the god of light and the god of darkness. Traditional Judaism and Christianity refer to it as a tension between God and Satan. Whatever you call it, there is a struggle in the universe between good and evil.

Now, not only is that struggle structured out somewhere in the external forces of the universe, it's structured in our own lives. Psychologists have tried to grapple with it in their way, and so they say various things. Sigmund Freud used to say that this tension is a tension between what he called the id and the superego.

But you know, some of us feel that it's a tension between God and man. And in every one of us this morning, there's a war going on. (*Yes, sir*) It's a civil war. (*Yes, sir*) I don't care who you are, I don't care where you live, there is a civil war going on in your life. (*Yes it is*) And every time you set out to be good, there's something pulling on you, telling you to be evil. It's going on in your life. (*Preach it*) Every time you set out to love, something keeps pulling on you, trying to get you to hate. (*Yes. Yes, sir*) Every time you set out to be kind and say nice things about people, something is pulling on you to be jealous and envious and to spread evil gossip about them. (*Yes. Preach it*) There's a civil war going on. There is a schizophrenia, as the psychologists or the psychiatrists would call it, going on within all of us. And there are times that all of us know somehow that there is a Mr. Hyde and a Dr. Jekyll in us. And we end up having to cry out with Ovid, the Latin poet, "I see and approve the better things of life, but the evil things I do." We end up having to agree with Plato that the human personality is like a charioteer with two headstrong horses, each wanting to go in different directions. Or sometimes we even have to end up crying out with Saint Augustine as he said in his *Confessions,* "Lord, make me pure, but not yet." (*Amen*) We end up crying out with the Apostle Paul, (*Preach it*) "The good that I would I do not: And the evil that I would not, that I do." Or we end up having to say with Goethe that "there's enough stuff in me to make both a gentleman and a rogue." (*All right. Amen*) There's a tension at the heart of human nature. (*Oh yeah*) And whenever we set out to dream our dreams and to build our temples, we must be honest enough to recognize it.

And this brings me to the basic point of the text. In the final analysis, God does not judge us by the separate incidents or the separate mistakes that we make, but by the total bent of our lives. In the final analysis, God knows (*Yes*) that his children are weak and they are frail. (*Yes, he does*) In the final analysis, what God requires is that your heart is right. (*Amen. Yes*) Salvation isn't reaching the destination of absolute morality, but it's being in the process and on the right road. (*Yes*)

There's a highway called Highway 80. I've marched on that highway from Selma, Alabama, to Montgomery. But I never will forget my first experience with Highway 80 was driving with Coretta and Ralph and Juanita Abernathy to California. We drove from Montgomery all the way to Los Angeles on Highway 80—it goes all the way out to Los Angeles. And you know, being a good man, being a good woman, does not mean that you've arrived in Los Angeles. It simply means that you're on Highway 80. (*Lord have mercy*) Maybe you haven't gotten as far as Selma, or maybe you haven't gotten as far as Meridian, Mississippi, or Monroe, Louisiana—that isn't the question. The question is whether you are on the right road. (*That's right*) Salvation is being on the right road, not having reached a destination.

Oh, we have to finally face the point that there is none good but the father. (*That's right*) But if you're on the right road, God has the power, (*Yes, sir*) and he has something called Grace. (*Yes, sir*) And he puts you where you ought to be.

Now, the terrible thing in life is to be trying to get to Los Angeles on Highway 78. That's when you are lost. (*Yes*) That sheep was lost, not merely because he was doing something wrong in that parable, but he was on the wrong road. (*Yes*) And he didn't even know where he was going; he became so involved in what he was doing, nibbling sweet grass, (*Make it plain*) that he got on the wrong road. (*Amen*) Salvation is being sure that you're on the right road. (*Yes. Preach it*) It is well— that's what I like about it—that it was within thine heart. (*Yes*)

Some weeks ago somebody was saying something to

me about a person that I have great, magnificent respect for. And they were trying to say something that didn't sound too good about his character, something he was doing. And I said, "Number one, I don't believe it. But number two, even if he is, (*Make it plain*) he's a good man because his heart is right." (*Amen*) And in the final analysis, God isn't going to judge him by that little separate mistake that he's making, (*No, sir*) because the bent of his life is right.

And the question I want to raise this morning with you: Is your heart right? (*Yes. Preach*) If your heart isn't right, fix it up today; get God to fix it up. (*Go ahead*) Get somebody to be able to say about you, "He may not have reached the highest height, (*Preach it*) he may not have realized all of his dreams, but he tried." (*Yes*) Isn't that a wonderful thing for somebody to say about you? "He tried to be a good man. (*Yes*) He tried to be a just man. He tried to be an honest man. (*Yes*) His heart was in the right place." (*Yes*) And I can hear a voice saying, crying out through the eternities, "I accept you. (*Preach it*) You are a recipient of my grace because it was in your heart. (*Yes*) And it is so well that it was within thine heart." (*Yes, sir*)

I don't know this morning about you, but I can make a testimony. (*Yes, sir. That's my life*) You don't need to go out this morning saying that Martin Luther King is a saint. Oh, no. (*Yes*) I want you to know this morning that I'm a sinner like all of God's children. But I want to be a good man. (*Yes. Preach it*) And I want to hear a voice saying to me one day, "I take you in and I bless you, because you try. (*Yes. Amen*) It is well (*Preach it*) that it was within thine heart." (*Yes*) What's in your heart this morning? (*Oh Lord*) If you get your heart right . . .*

Oh, this morning, if I can leave anything with you, let me urge you to be sure that you have a strong boat of faith. [*Laughter*] The winds are going to blow. (*Yes*) The storms of disappointment are coming. (*Yes*) The agonies and the anguishes of life are coming. (*Yes, sir*) And be sure that your boat is strong, and also be very sure that you have an anchor. (*Amen*) In times like these, you need an anchor. And be very sure that your anchor holds. (*Yes. Glory to God*)

It will be dark sometimes, and it will be dismal and trying, and tribulations will come. But if you have faith in the God that I'm talking about this morning, it doesn't matter. (*Yes*) For you can stand up amid the storms. And I say it to you out of experience this morning; yes, I've seen the lightning flash. (*Yes, sir*) I've heard the thunder roll. (*Yes*) I've felt sin-breakers dashing, trying to conquer my soul. But I heard the voice of Jesus, saying still to fight on. He promised never to leave me, (*Yes, sir*) never to leave me alone. (*Thank you, Jesus*) No, never alone. No, never alone. He promised never to leave me. Never to leave me alone. (*Glory to God*)

And when you get this faith, you can walk with your feet solid to the ground and your head to the air, and

---

*Recording interrupted.

you fear no man. (*Go ahead*) And you fear nothing that comes before you. (*Yes, sir*) Because you know that God is even in Crete. (*Amen*) If you ascend to the heavens, God is there. If you descend to hell, God is even there. If you take the wings of the morning and fly out to the uttermost parts of the sea, even God is there. Everywhere we turn we find him. We can never escape him.*

DELIVERED AT EBENEZER BAPTIST CHURCH, ATLANTA, GEORGIA, 3 MARCH 1968 [MLKEC]

---

*Recording ends.

# REMAINING AWAKE THROUGH A GREAT REVOLUTION

## INTRODUCTION BY ARCHBISHOP DESMOND TUTU

I had forgotten just how eloquent Dr. Martin Luther King was. Those splendid cadences are now lost to the world except through works such as this one. Very few could put words together in quite the way he had a knack for doing: "We have made of this world a neighborhood and yet we have not had the ethical commitment to make it a brotherhood." And how often have we quoted his beautiful saying about human community, "We must learn to live together as brothers or we will perish together as fools." Or heard him say, "Racial injustice is still the black man's burden and the white man's shame." Who could better his "The time is always ripe to do right"?

It is almost as if he were preaching that sermon for us today, for it is as apt today as it ever was nearly thirty years ago. We are undergoing another period of transition, when we could so easily become Rip Van Winkles sleeping through great revolutions because we had failed to develop the new attitudes, the new mental responses that the new situation demands. We have become so aware that this world has become a global village—a car accident in France throws the entire world into mourning—and yet we could still live as if this were not an increasingly interdependent universe we inhabit. When we could spend obscene amounts on weapons of death and destruction when just a minute fraction of those budgets of death would ensure that God's children everywhere would have clean water, adequate health care, enough to eat, a decent home and education. It is wonderful that Dr. Martin Luther King was so passionate in his opposition to war and so zealous for peace. And we give thanks that the international campaign to ban land mines has won the Nobel Peace Prize for 1997, because these awful things maim and kill long after the conflict is over.

He is as relevant as he ever was in his zeal for racial justice and equality. Eleven o'clock on a Sunday morning is still the most segregated hour in many racially diverse countries. And surely we do not want to sleep through the revolution of ending poverty.

I am sure he would have supported the call for the IMF and the World Bank to prepare for the new millennium by invoking the biblical principle of Jubilee, calling for the cancellation of the debt that so many poor countries carry. I give thanks for this remarkable man. Spiritual truth, it seems, is always relevant and apt. Thus it is not ultimately surprising to see just how applicable Dr. King's sermon in the National Cathedral in 1968 is to today's situation.

---

THE RIGHT REVEREND DESMOND TUTU, Anglican bishop of Johannesburg, was awarded the 1984 Nobel Peace Prize for his tireless efforts to end apartheid in South Africa. Reverend Tutu was also the first black secretary general of the interdenominational South African Council of Churches, and his sermons and speeches have been collected into two volumes, *Crying in the Wilderness* (1982) and *Hope and Suffering* (1984).

# REMAINING AWAKE
# THROUGH A GREAT
# REVOLUTION

I t is always a rich and re-
warding experience to take a brief break from our day-
to-day demands and the struggle for freedom and
human dignity and discuss the issues involved in that
struggle with concerned friends of goodwill all over
our nation. And certainly it is always a deep and meaningful experience to be in a worship service. And so for
many reasons, I'm happy to be here today.

I would like to use as a subject from which to preach
this morning: "Remaining Awake Through a Great
Revolution." The text for the morning is found in the
Book of Revelation. There are two passages there that
I would like to quote, in the sixteenth chapter of that
book: "Behold, I make all things new; former things
are passed away."

I am sure that most of you have read that arresting
little story from the pen of Washington Irving entitled
"Rip Van Winkle." The one thing that we usually remember about the story is that Rip Van Winkle slept
twenty years. But there is another point in that little

story that is almost completely overlooked. It was the sign in the end, from which Rip went up in the mountain for his long sleep.

When Rip Van Winkle went up into the mountains, the sign had a picture of King George the Third of England. When he came down twenty years later, the sign had a picture of George Washington, the first president of the United States. When Rip Van Winkle looked up at the picture of George Washington—and looking at the picture, he was amazed—he was completely lost. He knew not who he was.

And this reveals to us that the most striking thing about the story of Rip Van Winkle is not merely that Rip slept twenty years, but that he slept through a revolution. While he was peacefully snoring up in the mountain a revolution was taking place that at points would change the course of history—and Rip knew nothing about it. He was asleep. Yes, he slept through a revolution. And one of the great liabilities of life is that all too many people find themselves living amid a great period of social change, and yet they fail to develop the new attitudes, the new mental responses, that the new situation demands. They end up sleeping through a revolution.

There can be no gainsaying of the fact that a great revolution is taking place in the world today. In a sense it is a triple revolution: that is, a technological revolution, with the impact of automation and cybernation; then there is a revolution in weaponry, with the emergence of atomic and nuclear weapons of warfare; then there is a human rights revolution, with the freedom explosion that is taking place all over the world. Yes, we do live in a period where changes are taking place. And there is still the voice crying through the vista of time, saying, "Behold, I make all things new; former things are passed away."

Now, whenever anything new comes into history it brings with it new challenges and new opportunities. And I would like to deal with the challenges that we face today as a result of this triple revolution that is taking place in the world today.

First, we are challenged to develop a world perspective. No individual can live alone, no nation can live alone, and anyone who feels that he can live alone is sleeping through a revolution. The world in which we live is geographically one. The challenge that we face today is to make it one in terms of brotherhood.

Now, it is true that the geographical oneness of this age has come into being to a large extent through modern man's scientific ingenuity. Modern man through his scientific genius has been able to dwarf distance and place time in chains. And our jet planes have compressed into minutes distances that once took weeks and even months. All of this tell us that our world is a neighborhood.

Through our scientific and technological genius, we have made of this world a neighborhood and yet we have not had the ethical commitment to make of it a brotherhood. But somehow, and in some way, we have got to do this. We must all learn to live together as brothers or we will all perish together as fools. We are tied together in the single garment of destiny, caught in an inescapable network of mutuality. And whatever affects one directly affects all indirectly. For some strange reason I can never be what I ought to be until you are what you ought to be. And you can never be what you ought to be until I am what I ought to be. This is the way God's universe is made; this is the way it is structured.

John Donne caught it years ago and placed it in graphic terms: "No man is an island entire of itself. Every man is a piece of the continent, a part of the main." And he goes on toward the end to say, "Any man's death diminishes me because I am involved in mankind; therefore never send to know for whom the bell tolls; it tolls for thee." We must see this, believe this, and live by it if we are to remain awake through a great revolution.

Secondly, we are challenged to eradicate the last vestiges of racial injustice from our nation. I must say this morning that racial injustice is still the black man's burden and the white man's shame.

It is an unhappy truth that racism is a way of life for the vast majority of white Americans, spoken and unspoken, acknowledged and denied, subtle and sometimes not so subtle—the disease of racism permeates and poisons a whole body politic. And I can see nothing more urgent than for America to work passionately and unrelentingly—to get rid of the disease of racism.

Something positive must be done. Everyone must

share in the guilt as individuals and as institutions. The government must certainly share the guilt; individuals must share the guilt; even the church must share the guilt.

We must face the sad fact that at eleven o'clock on Sunday morning when we stand to sing "In Christ there is no East or West," we stand in the most segregated hour of America.

The hour has come for everybody, for all institutions of the public sector and the private sector, to work to get rid of racism. And now if we are to do it we must honestly admit certain things and get rid of certain myths that have constantly been disseminated all over our nation.

One is the myth of time. It is the notion that only time can solve the problem of racial injustice. And there are those who often sincerely say to the Negro and his allies in the white community, "Why don't you slow up? Stop pushing things so fast. Only time can solve the problem. And if you will just be nice and patient and continue to pray, in a hundred or two hundred years the problem will work itself out."

There is an answer to that myth. It is that time is neutral. It can be used either constructively or destructively. And I am sorry to say this morning that I am absolutely convinced that the forces of ill will in our nation, the extreme rightists of our nation—the people on the wrong side—have used time much more effectively than the forces of goodwill. And it may well be that we will have to repent in this generation. Not merely for the vitriolic words and the violent actions of the bad people, but for the appalling silence and indifference of the good people who sit around and say "Wait on time."

Somewhere we must come to see that human progress never rolls in on the wheels of inevitability. It comes through the tireless efforts and the persistent work of dedicated individuals who are willing to be co-workers with God. And without this hard work, time itself becomes an ally of the primitive forces of social stagnation. So we must help time and realize that the time is always ripe to do right.

Now, there is another myth that still gets around: It is a kind of overreliance on the bootstrap philosophy. There are those who still feel that if the Negro is to rise out of poverty, if the Negro is to rise out of the slum conditions, if he is to rise out of discrimination and segregation, he must do it all by himself. And so they say the Negro must lift himself by his own bootstraps.

They never stop to realize that no other ethnic group has been a slave on American soil. The people who say this never stop to realize that the nation made the black man's color a stigma. But beyond this they never stop to realize the debt that they owe a people who were kept in slavery two hundred and forty-four years.

In 1863 the Negro was told that he was free as a result of the Emancipation Proclamation being signed by Abraham Lincoln. But he was not given any land to make that freedom meaningful. It was something like keeping a person in prison for a number of years and suddenly discovering that that person is not guilty of the crime for which he was convicted. And you just go up to him and say, "Now you are free," but you don't give him any bus fare to get to town. You don't give him any money to get some clothes to put on his back or to get on his feet again in life.

Every court of jurisprudence would rise up against this, and yet this is the very thing that our nation did to the black man. It simply said, "You're free," and it left him there penniless, illiterate, not knowing what to do. And the irony of it all is that at the same time the nation failed to do anything for the black man, though . . . Congress was giving away millions of acres of land in the West and the Midwest. Which meant that it was willing to undergird its white peasants from Europe with an economic floor.

But not only did it give the land, it built land-grant colleges to teach them how to farm. Not only that, it provided county agents to further their expertise in farming; not only that, as the years unfolded it provided low interest rates so that they could mechanize their farms. And to this day thousands of these very persons are receiving millions of dollars in federal subsidies every year not to farm. And these are so often the very people who tell Negroes that they must lift themselves by their own bootstraps. It's all right to tell a man to lift himself by his own bootstraps, but it is a cruel jest to say to a bootless man that he ought to lift himself by his own bootstraps.

We must come to see that the roots of racism are very deep in our country, and there must be something positive and massive in order to get rid of all the effects of racism and the tragedies of racial injustice.

There is another thing closely related to racism that I would like to mention as another challenge. We are challenged to rid our nation and the world of poverty. Like a monstrous octopus, poverty spreads its nagging, prehensile tentacles into hamlets and villages all over our world. Two-thirds of the people of the world go to bed hungry tonight. They are ill-housed; they are ill-nourished; they are shabbily clad. I've seen it in Latin America; I've seen it in Africa; I've seen this poverty in Asia.

I remember some years ago Mrs. King and I journeyed to that great country known as India. And I never will forget the experience. It was a marvelous experience to meet and talk with the great leaders of India, to meet and talk with and to speak to thousands and thousands of people all over that vast country. These experiences will remain dear to me as long as the cords of memory shall lengthen.

But I say to you this morning, my friends, there were those depressing moments. How can one avoid being depressed when he sees with his own eyes evidence of millions of people going to bed hungry at night? How can one avoid being depressed when he sees with his own eyes God's children sleeping on the sidewalks at night? In Bombay more than a million people sleep on the sidewalks every night. In Calcutta more than six hundred thousand sleep on the sidewalks every night. They have no beds to sleep in; they have no houses to go in. How can one avoid being depressed when he discovers that out of India's population of more than five hundred million people, some four hundred and eighty million make an annual income of less than ninety dollars a year. And most of them have never seen a doctor or a dentist.

As I noticed these things, something within me cried out, "Can we in America stand idly by and not be concerned?" And an answer came: "Oh no!" Because the destiny of the United States is tied up with the destiny of India and every other nation. And I started thinking of the fact that we spend in America millions of dollars a day to store surplus food, and I said to myself, "I know where we can store that food free of charge—in the wrinkled stomachs of millions of God's children all over the world who go to bed hungry at night." And maybe we spend far too much of our national budget establishing military bases around the world rather than bases of genuine concern and understanding.

Not only do we see poverty abroad, I would remind you that in our own nation there are about forty million people who are poverty-stricken. I have seen them here and there. I have seen them in the ghettos of the North; I have seen them in the rural areas of the South; I have seen them in Appalachia. I have just been in the process of touring many areas of our country, and I must confess that in some situations I have literally found myself crying.

I was in Marks, Mississippi, the other day, which is in Quitman County, the poorest county in the United States. I tell you, I saw hundreds of little black boys and black girls walking the streets with no shoes to wear. I saw their mothers and fathers trying to carry on a little Head Start program, but they had no money. The federal government hadn't funded them, but they were trying to carry on. They raised a little money here and there; trying to get a little food to feed the children; trying to teach them a little something.

And I saw mothers and fathers who said to me not only were they unemployed, they didn't get any kind of income—no old-age pension, no welfare check, no anything. I said, "How do you live?" And they say, "Well, we go around, go around to the neighbors and ask them for a little something. When the berry season comes, we pick berries. When the rabbit season comes, we hunt and catch a few rabbits. And that's about it."

And I was in Newark and Harlem just this week. And I walked into the homes of welfare mothers. I saw them in conditions—no, not with wall-to-wall carpet, but wall-to-wall rats and roaches. I stood in an apartment and this welfare mother said to me, "The landlord will not repair this place. I've been here two years and he hasn't made a single repair." She pointed out the walls with all the ceiling falling through. She showed me the holes where the rats came in. She said, "Night after night we have to stay awake to keep the rats and roaches from getting to the children." I said, "How much do you pay for this apartment?" She said, "A hundred and twenty-five dollars." I looked, and I thought, and said to myself, "It isn't worth sixty dollars." Poor people are forced to pay more for less. Living in conditions day in and day out where the whole area is constantly drained without being replenished. It becomes a kind of domestic colony. And the tragedy is, so often these forty million people are invisible because America is so affluent, so rich. Because our expressways carry us from the ghetto, we don't see the poor.

Jesus told a parable one day, and he reminded us that a man went to hell because he didn't see the poor. His name was Dives. He was a rich man. And there was a man by the name of Lazarus who was a poor man, but not only was he poor, he was sick. Sores were all over his body, and he was so weak that he could hardly move. But he managed to get to the gate of Dives every day, wanting just to have the crumbs that would fall from his table. And Dives did nothing about it. And the parable ends saying, "Dives went to hell, and there was a fixed gulf now between Lazarus and Dives."

There is nothing in that parable that said Dives went to hell because he was rich. Jesus never made a universal indictment against all wealth. It is true that one day a rich young ruler came to him, and he advised him to sell all, but in that instance Jesus was prescribing individual surgery and not setting forth a universal diagnosis. And if you will look at that parable with all of its symbolism, you will remember that a conversation took place between heaven and hell, and on the other end of that long-distance call between heaven and hell was Abraham in heaven talking to Dives in hell.

Now, Abraham was a very rich man. If you go back to the Old Testament, you see that he was the richest man of his day, so it was not a rich man in hell talking with a poor man in heaven; it was a little millionaire in hell talking with a multimillionaire in heaven. Dives didn't go to hell because he was rich; Dives didn't realize that his wealth was his opportunity. It was his opportunity to bridge the gulf that separated him from his brother Lazarus. Dives went to hell because he passed by Lazarus every day and he never really saw him. He went to hell because he allowed his brother to become invisible. Dives went to hell because he maximized the minimum and minimized the maximum. Indeed, Dives went to hell because he sought to be a conscientious objector in the war against poverty.

And this can happen to America, the richest nation in the world—and nothing's wrong with that—this is America's opportunity to help bridge the gulf between the haves and the have-nots. The question is whether America will do it. There is nothing new about poverty. What is new is that we now have the techniques and the resources to get rid of poverty. The real question is whether we have the will.

In a few weeks some of us are coming to Washington to see if the will is still alive or if it's alive in this nation. We are coming to Washington in a Poor People's Campaign. Yes, we are going to bring the tired, the poor, the huddled masses. We are going to bring those who have known long years of hurt and neglect. We are going to bring those who have come to feel that life is a long and desolate corridor with no exit signs. We are going to bring children and adults and old people, people who have never seen a doctor or a dentist in their lives.

We are not coming to engage in any histrionic gesture. We are not coming to tear up Washington. We are coming to demand that the government address itself to the problem of poverty. We read one day, "We hold these truths to be self-evident, that all men are created equal, that they are endowed by their Creator with certain inalienable Rights, that among these are Life, Liberty, and the pursuit of Happiness." But if a man doesn't have a job or an income, he has neither life nor liberty nor the possibility for the pursuit of happiness. He merely exists.

We are coming to ask America to be true to the huge promissory note that it signed years ago. And we are coming to engage in dramatic nonviolent action, to call attention to the gulf between promise and fulfillment; to make the invisible visible.

Why do we do it this way? We do it this way because it is our experience that the nation doesn't move around questions of genuine equality for the poor and for black people until it is confronted massively, dramatically in terms of direct action.

Great documents are here to tell us something should be done. We met here some years ago in the White House conference on civil rights. And we came out with the same recommendations that we will be demanding in our campaign here, but nothing has been done. The president's commission on technology, automation, and economic progress recommended these things some time ago. Nothing has been done. Even the urban coalition of mayors of most of the cities of our country and the leading businessmen have said these things should be done. Nothing has been done. The Kerner Commission came out with its report just a few days ago and then made specific recommendations. Nothing has been done.

And I submit that nothing will be done until people of goodwill put their bodies and their souls in motion. And it will be the kind of soul force brought into being as a result of this confrontation that I believe will make the difference.

Yes, it will be a Poor People's Campaign. This is the question facing America. Ultimately a great nation is a compassionate nation. America has not met its obligations and its responsibilities to the poor.

One day we will have to stand before the God of history and we will talk in terms of things we've done. Yes, we will be able to say we built gargantuan bridges to span the seas, we built gigantic buildings to kiss the skies. Yes, we made our submarines to penetrate oceanic depths. We brought into being many other things with our scientific and technological power.

It seems that I can hear the God of history saying, "That was not enough! But I was hungry, and ye fed me not. I was naked, and ye clothed me not. I was devoid of a decent sanitary house to live in, and ye provided no shelter for me. And consequently, you cannot enter the kingdom of greatness. If ye do it unto the least of these, my brethren, ye do it unto me." That's the question facing America today.

I want to say one other challenge that we face is simply that we must find an alternative to war and bloodshed. Anyone who feels—and there are still a lot of people who feel that way—that war can solve the social problems facing mankind is sleeping through a great revolution. President Kennedy said on one occasion, "Mankind must put an end to war or war will put an end to mankind." The world must hear this. I pray God that America will hear this before it is too late, because today we're fighting a war.

I am convinced that it is one of the most unjust wars that has ever been fought in the history of the world. Our involvement in the war in Vietnam has torn up the Geneva Accord. It has strengthened the military-industrial complex; it has strengthened the forces of reaction in our nation. It has put us against the self-determination of a vast majority of the Vietnamese people, and put us in the position of protecting a corrupt regime that is stacked against the poor.

It has played havoc with our domestic destinies. This day we are spending five hundred thousand dollars to kill every Vietcong soldier. Every time we kill one we spend about five hundred thousand dollars, while we spend only fifty-three dollars a year for every person characterized as poverty-stricken in the so-called poverty program, which is not even a good skirmish against poverty.

Not only that, it has put us in a position of appearing to the world as an arrogant nation. And here we are ten thousand miles away from home, fighting for the so-called freedom of the Vietnamese people, when we have not even put our own house in order. And we force young black men and young white men to fight and kill in brutal solidarity. Yet when they come back home they can't hardly live on the same block together.

The judgment of God is upon us today. And we could go right down the line and see that something must be done—and something must be done quickly. We have alienated ourselves from other nations so we end up morally and politically isolated in the world. There is not a single major ally of the United States of America that would dare send a troop to Vietnam, and so the only friends that we have now are a few client-nations like Taiwan, Thailand, South Korea, and a few others.

This is where we are. "Mankind must put an end to war or war will put an end to mankind," and the best way to start is to put an end to war in Vietnam, because if it continues, we will inevitably come to the point of confronting China, which could lead the whole world to nuclear annihilation.

It is no longer a choice, my friends, between violence and nonviolence. It is either nonviolence or nonexistence. And the alternative to disarmament, the alternative to a greater suspension of nuclear tests, the alternative to strengthening the United Nations and thereby disarming the whole world, may well be a civilization plunged into the abyss of annihilation, and our earthly habitat would be transformed into an inferno that even the mind of Dante could not imagine.

This is why I felt the need of raising my voice against that war and working wherever I can to arouse the conscience of our nation on it. I remember so well when I first took a stand against the war in Vietnam. The critics took me on and they had their say in the most negative and sometimes most vicious way.

One day a newsman came to me and said, "Dr. King, don't you think you're going to have to stop now opposing the war and move more in line with the administration's policy? As I understand it, it has hurt the budget of your organization, and people who once respected you have lost respect for you. Don't you feel that you've really got to change your position?" I looked at him and I had to say, "Sir, I'm sorry you don't know me. I'm not a consensus leader. I do not determine what is right and wrong by looking at the budget of the Southern Christian Leadership Conference. I've not taken a sort of Gallup poll of the majority opinion." Ultimately a genuine leader is not a searcher for consensus but a molder of consensus.

On some positions, cowardice asks the question, Is it expedient? And then expedience comes along and asks the question, Is it politic? Vanity asks the question, Is it popular? Conscience asks the question, Is it right?

There comes a time when one must take the position that is neither safe nor politic nor popular, but he must do it because conscience tells him it is right. I believe today that there is a need for all people of goodwill to come with a massive act of conscience and say in the words of the old Negro spiritual, "We ain't gonna study war no more." This is the challenge facing modern man.

Let me close by saying that we have difficult days ahead in the struggle for justice and peace, but I will not yield to a politic of despair. I'm going to maintain hope as we come to Washington in this campaign. The cards are stacked against us. This time we will really confront a Goliath. God grant that we will be that David of truth set out against the Goliath of injustice, the Goliath of neglect, the Goliath of refusing to deal with the problems, and go on with the determination to make America the truly great America that it is called to be.

I say to you that our goal is freedom, and I believe we are going to get there because however much she strays away from it, the goal of America is freedom. Abused and scorned though we may be as a people, our destiny is tied up in the destiny of America.

Before the Pilgrim fathers landed at Plymouth, we were here. Before Jefferson etched across the pages of history the majestic words of the Declaration of Independence, we were here. Before the beautiful words of "The Star-Spangled Banner" were written, we were here.

For more than two centuries our forebears labored here without wages. They made cotton king, and they built the homes of their masters in the midst of the most humiliating and oppressive conditions. And yet out of a bottomless vitality they continued to grow and develop. If the inexpressible cruelties of slavery couldn't stop us, the opposition that we now face will surely fail.

We're going to win our freedom because both the sacred heritage of our nation and the eternal will of the almighty God are embodied in our echoing demands. And so, however dark it is, however deep the angry feelings are, and however violent explosions are, I can still sing "We Shall Overcome."

We shall overcome because the arc of the moral universe is long, but it bends toward justice.

We shall overcome because Carlyle is right: "No lie can live forever."

We shall overcome because William Cullen Bryant is right: "Truth, crushed to earth, will rise again."

We shall overcome because James Russell Lowell is right: As we were singing earlier today,

Truth forever on the scaffold,
Wrong forever on the throne.
Yet that scaffold sways the future.
And behind the dim unknown stands God,
Within the shadow keeping watch above his own.

With this faith we will be able to hew out of the mountain of despair the stone of hope. With this faith we will be able to transform the jangling discords of our nation into a beautiful symphony of brotherhood.

Thank God for John, who centuries ago out on a lonely, obscure island called Patmos caught vision of a new Jerusalem descending out of heaven from God, who heard a voice saying, "Behold, I make all things new; former things are passed away."

God grant that we will be participants in this newness and this magnificent development. If we will but do it, we will bring about a new day of justice and brotherhood and peace. And that day the morning stars will sing together and the sons of God will shout for joy. God bless you.

DELIVERED AT THE NATIONAL CATHEDRAL, WASHINGTON, D.C., 31 MARCH 1968 [CONGRESSIONAL RECORD, 9 APRIL 1968]

# MATERIAL OMITTED FROM THE SERMONS

Dr. King's introductory comments to relevant sermons are included here.

## REDISCOVERING LOST VALUES

Reverend Simmons, platform associates, members and friends of Second Baptist Church, I need not pause to say how happy I am to be here this morning, and to be a part of this worship service. It is certainly with a deal of humility that I stand in this pulpit so rich in tradition and history. Second Baptist Church, as you know, has the reputation of being one of the great churches of our nation, and it is certainly a challenge for me to stand here this morning, to be in the pulpit of Reverend Banks and of a people who are so great and rich in tradition.

I'm not exactly a stranger in the city of Detroit, for I have been here several times before. And I remember back in about 1944 or 1945, somewhere back in there, that I came to Second Baptist Church for the first time—I think that was the year that the National Baptist Convention met here. And of course I have a lot of relatives in this city, so that Detroit is really something of a second home for me, and I don't feel too much a stranger here this morning. So it is indeed a pleasure and a privilege for me to be in this city this morning, and to be here to worship with you in the absence of your very fine and noble pastor, Dr. Banks.

## LOVING YOUR ENEMIES

I am forced to preach under something of a handicap this morning. In fact, I saw the doctor before coming to church. And he said that it would be best for me to stay in bed this morning. And I insisted that I would have to come to preach. So he allowed me to come out with one stipulation, and that is that I would not come in the pulpit until time to preach, and that after, that I would immediately go back home and get in bed. So I'm going to try to follow his instructions.

I want to use as a subject from which to preach this morning a very familiar subject, and it is familiar to you because I have preached from this subject twice before to my knowing in this pulpit. I try to make it a—something of a custom or tradition to preach from this passage of scripture at least once a year, adding new insights that I develop along the way out of new experiences as I give these messages. Although the content is, the basic content is the same, new insights and new experiences naturally make for new illustrations.

# GUIDELINES FOR A CONSTRUCTIVE CHURCH

I would like to preach from the subject: "Guidelines for a Constructive Church." Over the last several weeks now, we've been reading a good deal in our newspapers about guidelines. Now, this word has been applied basically to the public school systems across our nation, particularly in the South. The Supreme Court of our nation rendered a decision back in 1954 declaring segregation in the public schools unconstitutional. And that next year, in 1955, it came back stating that every school district was to integrate "with all deliberate speed." And yet we came into 1966 with the terrible realization that only 5.2 percent of the Negro students of the South had been placed in integrated schools, which meant in substance that we haven't made 1 percent progress a year. And if it continued at that pace it would take another ninety-six years to integrate the public schools of the South.

And so the Department of Education decided that the process had to be speeded up on the basis of the Civil Rights Bill of 1964. And this department decided to set forth certain basic guidelines that had to be followed. The guidelines stated in substance that the process of integration had to be speeded up; that all grades had to be integrated; that even faculties had to be integrated. And this plan, or these guidelines, was submitted to every school district, and that school district had to decide whether it would follow the guidelines. If it refused to follow the guidelines then federal funds would be cut off. If it complied with the guidelines then federal funds would be continued. And so today there is a great discussion all over the educational world and the public school system about whether a school district or a school board will follow the guidelines.

## WHY JESUS CALLED A MAN A FOOL

To my good friend Dr. Wells, to the officers and members of Mount Pisgah Missionary Baptist Church, my Christian brothers and sisters, I can assure you that it would take me the rest of my days to live up to that eloquent, beautiful introduction just made by this charming member of your congregation. It makes me feel very humble. And such encouraging words give me renewed courage and vigor to carry on in the struggle for freedom and human dignity. I'm deeply grateful to your esteemed pastor for extending the invitation for me to be with you. And I'm grateful to him for the support that he has given me in my humble efforts. You know, I learned a long time ago that you can't make it by yourself in this world. You need friends; you need somebody to pat you on the back; you need somebody to give you consolation in the darkest hours. And I'm so grateful to all of the friends in the city of Chicago and to the many ministers of the gospel who have given me that kind of support and encouragement.

## REMAINING AWAKE THROUGH A GREAT REVOLUTION

I need not pause to say how very delighted I am to be here this morning, to have the opportunity of standing in this very great and significant pulpit. And I do want to express my deep personal appreciation to Dean Sayre and all of the cathedral clergy for extending the invitation.

## SOURCE ABBREVIATIONS

[SdBCC] Second Baptist Church Collection, Detroit, Michigan
[MLKP] Martin Luther King, Jr., Papers, Boston University
[MLKEC] Martin Luther King, Jr., Estate Collection, Atlanta, Georgia

# ACKNOWLEDGMENTS

*Knock at Midnight* is an outgrowth of the King Papers Project's ongoing effort to produce an authoritative fourteen-volume edition of King's most significant correspondence, sermons, speeches, published writings, and unpublished manuscripts. The Martin Luther King, Jr., Center for Nonviolent Social Change, Inc., initiated this long-term documentary research and publication venture, which is being conducted in association with the King Estate, Stanford University, Emory University, and the University of California Press. Major finanical supporters of the project include the National Endowment for the Humanities, the National Historical Publications and Records Commission, and the Lilly Endowment. The editors wish to thank all the individuals associated with these institutions who have assisted in our efforts to assemble the extant recordings and transcripts of King's sermons.

In particular, this book results from the determined efforts of Dexter King, Chariman, President, and CEO of the King Center, and Phillip Jones, Chairman and CEO of Intellectual Properties Management (IPM), to expose the King Papers Project's scholarly research to a broader audience. Their help, along with the assistance of King Center founder Coretta Scott King, has greatly increased the amount of available documentary materials regarding Martin Luther King, Jr. Tricia Harris of IPM helped coordinate this project. This book is the first fruit of a continuing collaboration that will enhance popular understanding of King's life and thought.

The staff of Warner Books also provided necessary assistance to insure that this book was produced with care as well as dispatch. We thank especially our editor, Airié Dekidjiev, as well as Judith McGuinn and Maja Thomas of the Audio Books division.

Finally, we express appreciation for the support we have received from the staff of the King Papers Project, including managing editor Susan Carson, project administrator Francine Marsh-Davis, and research assistants Adrienne Clay and Kerry Taylor. Numerous researchers were involved in assembling and cataloging King-related documents and assisting in the difficult task of producing accurate transcripts of audio recordings that were more than thirty years old. The contribution of Emory University doctoral student Kris Sheppard was especially important in producing the transcriptions in this book. We appreciate the assistance of Robin Brooks of the King Center, who facilitated our efforts to obtain audio recordings. Finally, we also thank the student researchers in our Summer 1997 King Fellows Program, including Brandi Clay Brimmer, Joy Clinkscales, Andrew Davidson, Barbara Ifejika, and Hanan Aisha Hardy.

***

Intellectual Properties Management (IPM) wishes to thank the King family for their support of the IPM/Warner Books joint venture. Special thanks to Coretta Scott King and Dexter Scott King for their invaluable input into *A Knock at Midnight*. IPM also wishes to thank Laurence Kirshbaum, Maureen Egen, and the entire Warner Books staff for their dedication and partnership.

***

The King family wishes to thank Intellectual Properties Management for its continued support and vision for the King legacy. They also wish to thank all of the introduction writers, editors, and everyone involved in the preparation of *A Knock at Midnight*.